KNITTING
without
NEEDLES

KNITTING WITHOUT NEEDLES

A Stylish Introduction to
Finger and Arm Knitting

Anne Weil

POTTER
CRAFT

NEW YORK

Published in the United States by Potter Craft, an
imprint of the Crown Publishing Group, a division of
Penguin Random House LLC, New York.
www.crownpublishing.com
www.pottercraft.com

POTTER CRAFT and colophon are registered
trademarks of Penguin Random House LLC.

Library of Congress cataloging-in-publication data
is available upon request.

ISBN 978-0-8041-8652-0
eBook ISBN 978-0-8041-8653-7

Printed in China

Text design by Rae Ann Spitzenberger
Photographs by Lucy Schaeffer and Jessica Peterson
Styling by Brittany Jepsen and Pam Morris
How-to photography by Trisha Zemp
Cover design by Jessie Bright
Cover photographs by Jessica Peterson

10 9 8 7 6 5 4 3 2 1

First Edition

to sandy, charlie, baillie & allie, for
filling my heart to the very brim and
helping make my dreams come true
and to my dad, who instilled in me the
value of hard work and the belief that
i could do and be anything i want in life

CONTENTS

Introduction | 9

WEAR

LIVE

PLAY

HOW-TO

INTRODUCTION

Making something beautiful with my hands . . . this feeling brings me more joy than just about anything else in the world. That delight inspired me to begin my blog, *Flax & Twine*, in 2011. I needed more of that beauty-making bliss in my life.

Arm knitting and finger knitting are two of the purest expressions of how capable, creative hands can transform even the most mundane materials into works of beauty. I literally giggle sometimes that all the lovely projects in this book were made only with hands, no knitting needles required! From playful garments to bold accessories to chic home goods, this book proves that beautiful things are always—quite literally—at your fingertips.

As my blog started growing, along with my children, my family rediscovered finger knitting. As a child, I had learned to finger knit, and my love for it came rushing back. Weaving yarn by hand seemed to bring the kids (ages five, six, and seven at the time) the same satisfaction that it brought me. We made piles and piles and, literally, miles of finger-knit strands. But what in the world were we to do with it? I started designing finger-knitting projects that I thought were beautiful and found a huge demand for quality projects. In addition to a basic how-to, you'll learn finger-knitting techniques I've developed that open up a world of possibilities for this craft. No longer bound to the typical finger-knit "tube"

or "cord," now you can create projects more sophisticated than you thought possible.

Arm knitting was the next natural progression. No need to fuss with a hook or a pair of needles. You need only what you were born with and a little (or maybe a lot) of yarn. The modern shift in scale became a new obsession and drove me to become a pioneer in this new craft. Most arm knitting techniques are based on traditional knitting, but many beginners find that knitting on their arms is a friendlier, faster introduction to the skill. With these projects, you'll discover (or rediscover) how vibrant and fresh knitting can look when you work on a larger scale with lush, lofty yarns.

Hands of all ages can make the projects in this book, but don't be fooled by their child friendliness. These patterns are design driven, progressive, and shamelessly simple in their style, rendered in my signature warm, springy color palette. You can expect lots of modern, easy-to-make gifts, stunning additions to your wardrobe, and luxe home goods that are striking but playful, streamlined but charming. Best of all, every project is accompanied by easy-to-follow step-by-step photos.

Now it's time to dig in! I hope you enjoy making these items as much as I have. May this book bring joy to your happy handmade life!

xoxo, anne

CHAPTER 1

WEAR

From plush and lush to light and delicate, these swoon-worthy arm- and finger-knit accessories will have your friends asking, "Where'd you get that?" Lucky for you (and them!) these seemingly intricate creations are actually easy to make, which means you can surprise them with a gorgeous gift by tomorrow.

INFINITY COWL

I first fell in love with arm knitting when I discovered how a simple shift in scale could completely transform traditional knitting. The drama and loft charmed me from the start. Playing with yarn size and weight will result in a range of styles, from a lighter scarf perfect for the shoulder season to an impossibly cozy cowl you'll love diving into in the depths of winter.

materials

SLIM COWL (TAN): 348 yd (318m) of "slim" super-bulky yarn, (**6**), combining 4 x 87-yard (79.5m) lengths. The traditional knitting gauge for "slim" super-bulky is 2.75 sts per inch.

MID COWL (BLUE): 270 yd (247m) of "mid" super-bulky yarn, (**6**), combining 3 x 90-yard (82m) lengths. The traditional knitting gauge for "mid" super-bulky is 2.25–2.5 sts per inch.

BIG COWL (WHITE): 270 yd (247m) of "big" super-bulky yarn, (**6**), combining 3 x 90-yard (82m) lengths. The traditional knitting gauge for "big" super-bulky is 1.75–2.0 sts per inch.

» See pages 140–145 for an explanation of super-bulky yarns.

yarn used

SLIM COWL (TAN): 4 skeins Purl Soho Super Soft Merino in Sea Salt, 87 yd (79.5m), 3½ oz (100g), 100% Peruvian merino wool

MID COWL (BLUE): 3 skeins Madelinetosh ASAP in Mica, 90 yd (82m), 4½ oz (127g), 100% superwash merino wool

BIG COWL (WHITE): 6 skeins Blue Sky Alpaca Bulky in Polar Bear, 45 yd (41m), 3½ oz (100g), 50% alpaca, 50% wool

sizes & measurements

12 (13, 15)" (30.5cm [33cm, 38cm]) wide, 62" (157.5cm) long before looping

» Measurements will vary slightly based on your arm size, tension, and yarn choice.

» The length is the same for each cowl because you simply stop arm knitting when the piece reaches your desired length.

yarn preparation

For the Slim Cowl, hold 4 strands together to create full stitches like the sample. For the Mid and Big Cowls, hold 3 strands together to make the yarn. (See Arm-Knitting Yarn Preparation, page 182.)

1. Cast on 10 stitches to your right arm, holding 3 or 4 strands (see Yarn Preparation, above) together as your yarn.

2. Knit until the piece measures 62" (157.5cm) from the cast-on edge, adding a new yarn skein if necessary (page 170).

3. Bind off 10 stitches, leaving at least 1 yd (0.9m) of remaining yarn for seaming.

4. Lay the piece out flat, with the "wrong side" (purl side) facing up (**A**). Bring the 2 short ends of the rectangle together, forming a circle, with the right side of the cowl facing up (**B**). Use the remaining tail and mattress stitch (page 181) to seam the 2 ends together.

5. Weave in all loose ends.

STATEMENT NECKLACE

PROJECT TYPE
finger knitting

SKILL LEVEL
beginner

. . . .

TECHNIQUES

Casting on.....................148

Four-finger knitting......148

Binding off 150

Weaving in ends 154

Tightening strand
   ends........................155

Meet your newest conversation piece (psst . . . you can wear it two ways!). The secret to making it especially compliment worthy? A fabulous variegated yarn. Beautiful metal jump rings, a chain, and a clasp are easier to add than you may first believe, and they elevate humble finger knitting into a stunning showstopper.

materials

18 yd (16.5m) of worsted-weight yarn, (**4**), combining 3 x 6-yard (5.5m) lengths

4 jump rings

Chain, approximately 18" (45.5cm) long

Jewelry clasp

tools

Needle-nose pliers

Ruler or tape measure

Wire cutters

yarn used

1 skein Manos del Uruguay Clasica in Caribe, 138 yd (126m), 3½ oz (100g), 100% merino wool

sizes & measurements

Knit piece is 1½" (3.8cm) wide, 7" (18cm) long

yarn preparation

Measure and cut three 6-yd (5.5m) strands of yarn. Combine these 3 strands to create the yarn for the project.

note

» If you have 6 yd (5.5m) of a "slim" or "mid" super-bulky yarn left over from another project, you can finger knit this necklace using a single strand. (See pages 140–145 for an explanation of yarn weights.)

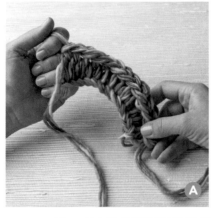

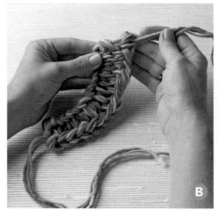

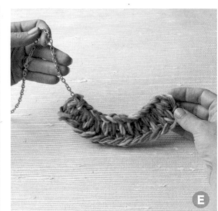

1. Leave a 12" (30.5cm) tail and cast on a four-finger knit strand.

2. Knit 14 rows, or until the piece measures approximately 7" (18cm) long (**A**).

. . . .

Tip: Do not pull on the cast-on tail of the finger knitting, which will roll the sides of the knit fabric in toward each other, forming a tube. If you don't pull the end, the piece will remain flat from side to side; however, the beginning and the end of the strand will naturally start to curl toward each other, like a smile, which is what you want.

. . . .

3. Bind off the strand without pulling tight so that the end of the necklace matches the rest of the piece (**B**).

4. Bring the working yarn through the last stitch to the knit side (**C**). Weave the yarn end into the knit side, hiding it as you go (**D**). Trim the end.

5. Return to the beginning of the finger-knit strand and tighten up the beginning of the piece to make it even with the rest of the strand (see page 155). Weave in the end and trim.

6. Using wire cutters, cut 2 pieces of chain to 7" (18cm), or desired length.

7. Place the necklace with the purl side facing up and curving like a smile. Using needle-nose pliers, open a jump ring, thread one piece of chain on it, and run the jump ring through the small top corner stitch of the necklace. Close the jump ring with needle-nose pliers, making sure the ring ends match up exactly as it closes (E). Repeat on the other side of the necklace.

8. Using the pliers, open another jump ring and loop it through the end of one of the chain pieces and one of the clasp pieces. Close the jump ring with the pliers. Repeat on the other side of the necklace (F).

Tip: I designed this necklace to be worn with the purl side facing out as shown below. For a different look, flip it to the knit side as shown on page 16.

DOUBLE-STRAND HEADBAND

These sweet finger-knit strands look perfectly charming in messy tresses on a lazy Saturday morning. The headband delivers color and texture with a side of effortless elegance. Or, if you're truly feeling lazy and in need of a quick project, skip the sewing part and secure the strands in your hair with a bobby pin or two.

PROJECT TYPE
finger knitting

SKILL LEVEL
intermediate

. . . .

TECHNIQUES
Casting on.....................151
Two-finger knitting 151
Binding off 151
Weaving in ends 154

materials

27 yd (25m) of worsted-weight yarn, (**4**), combining 3 x 9-yard (8.2m) lengths

10" (25.5cm) of cotton ribbon, ⅝" (16mm) wide

Thread color coordinated to the ribbon

6" (15cm) of elastic, ¼" (6mm) wide

tools

Scissors

Straight pins

Sewing needle or sewing machine

Safety pin

yarn used

1 skein Alchemy Kozmos in Turquoise Pool, 119 yd (109m), 1.6 oz (45g), 30% silk, 26% mohair, 13% wool, 31% cotton

sizes & measurements

1" (2.5cm) wide when strands are side by side, 22" (56cm) circumference or sized to fit

yarn preparation

Measure and cut three 9-yd (8.2m) strands of yarn. Combine these 3 strands together to create the yarn for this project.

1. Leaving a 10" (25.5cm) tail, cast on and finger knit a two-finger strand for 35 rows, or until it measures about 17" (43cm).

2. Bind off, leaving a 10" (25.5cm) tail (**A**).

3. Repeat steps 1 and 2 for the next strand.

4. Line up the strands side by side. Tie a knot where the finger knitting stops, bringing the 2 strands together. Repeat on the other end (**B**).

5. Cut 2 lengths of cotton ribbon to 4¾" (12cm). Fold the ribbon under ¼" (6mm) at both ends. Press this ¼" (6mm) fold hard with your fingers a few times so that it stays in the folded position.

6. Place the ribbons together with the folded sides facing each other and pin (**C**).

7. Sew a ⅛" (3mm) seam down both sides of the ribbon. If using a sewing machine, backstitch at each end. If hand sewing, reinforce the ends with a few extra stitches. Set aside.

8. Trim the yarn tails coming from the end of both strands about ¼" (6mm) from the knot.

9. Pin a 6" (15cm) piece of elastic to one end of the finger-knit strands, overlapping the elastic and the finger-knit strands by ½" (13mm). Sew across over the overlap of the strands and the knot 3 or 4 times to secure. (The stitching will be hidden underneath the ribbon sleeve, so it doesn't really matter how it looks.)

10. Attach a safety pin to the free end of the elastic. Thread it through the ribbon sleeve (**D**).

11. Pull on the elastic until you bring the attachment point and the beginning ¾" (2cm) of finger-knit strands into the sleeve.

12. Sew across the end of the sleeve (which encloses finger-knit strands and elastic) with a ⅛" (3mm) seam allowance to secure.

13. Position the headband on your head and pull the elastic to the other end of the finger-knit strands. Measure how tight you want the headband to be by keeping your fingers

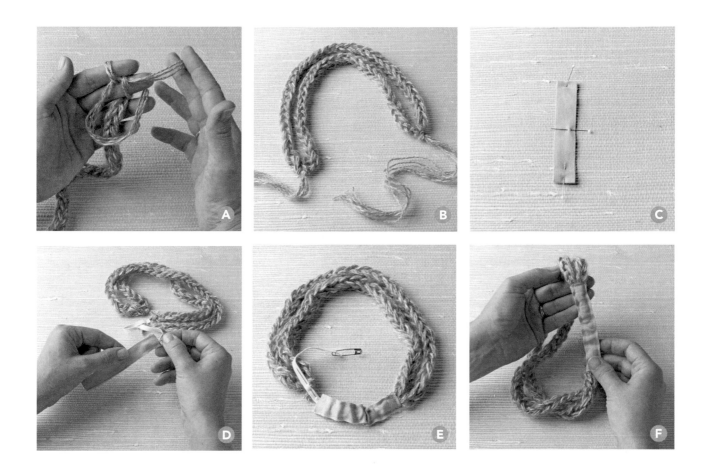

on this spot on the elastic. Pin it to the other ends of the finger-knit strands (E); about 2"– 2½" (5cm–6.5cm) between the attachment points. Make sure that the headband strands aren't twisted. Sew back and forth across this attachment point 3 or 4 times to secure.

15. Trim the elastic ¼" (6mm) from the stitching. Use the head of the safety pin to push the overlap and cast-on ends of the finger-knit strands into the ribbon sleeve. Sew across the end of the sleeve with a ⅛" (3mm) seam allowance (F). Trim all thread ends.

HEMP TWINE NECKLACE

Twine holds a special part in my heart. I included the word in my blog name not only because of its natural beauty as a fiber but also because of the sense of community and relationship the word implies to me. Finger-knit twine complements a summer dress for a clean, timeless look, or try gold or silver wire instead for a different style altogether.

materials

16 yd (15m) of hemp twine or stiff fingering-weight yarn, **1**

16 yd (15m) of embroidery thread

Glue (Fray Block dries quickly and clearly)

Thread in color to match embroidery thread

Decorative button (exact size isn't critical; choose as desired)

tools

Scissors

Sewing needle

materials used

1 skein Fingering Weight Crochet Hemp in Bleached, 1,655 yd (1,513m), 16 oz (454g), 100% pure hemp

1 skein DMC size 5 Color Variations embroidery thread in color 4040, 27 yd (25m), 100% cotton

sizes & measurements

2½" (6.5cm) wide from top strand to bottom, 22" (56cm) long

yarn preparation

Measure and cut three 5⅓ yd (4.9m) strands of hemp.

note:

» When making a necklace or any finger knitting that will be seen up close, it is important to be careful with craftsmanship. To get consistent tension and nicely finished ends, work mid-finger as opposed to at the bottom of your fingers.

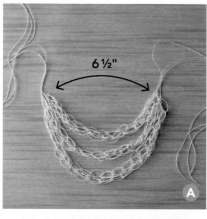

6½"

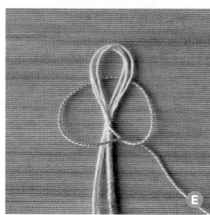

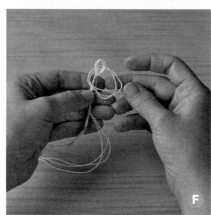

1. Begin a four-finger knit strand, leaving an 18" (45.5cm) tail. Pull the tail taut after the first row to tighten the beginning. Keep the working yarn for this first row fairly tight as you knit. Knit for approximately 17 rows, or until the strand measures 12½" (32cm).

2. Bind off this strand, pulling the tail slowly through the loops so that the stitches close evenly. Cut remaining yarn so there is an 18" (45.5cm) tail.

3. In the same manner, finger knit an 11½" (29cm) four-finger strand (approximately 15 rows). Bind off slowly. Leave an 18" (45.5cm) tail.

4. Finger knit a 10½" (26.5cm) four-finger strand (approximately 13 rows). Bind off slowly and leave an 18" (45.5cm) tail.

5. On a flat surface, line up the strands in increasing-length order, with the shortest at the top, matching the finger-knit ends. Stagger them just slightly so that they will taper nicely when wrapped. Evenly space the strands and arrange so that the ends are about 6½" (16.5cm) apart (**A**).

6. Knot the 3 strands together (**B**) at both ends, making an effort to minimize bulk. Lay the strands down to make sure they are still in order and are untwisted—just as you would want them to lie on your neck.

7. Lay the end of the embroidery thread parallel along the necklace strand starting 2" (5cm) up from the knotted strands and heading down toward the body of the necklace. Twist the embroidery thread in a loop, with the tail coming out from underneath the top of the loop, making a half hitch, and bring it over the necklace ends and the bulk of strands you are holding (C). Tighten the half hitch below the knot. Create another half hitch over the twine and ends. Pull tight.

8. Now, carefully begin wrapping the embroidery thread around the end of the strands, layering the thread on top of the prior wrap as you go (D). Do this by holding the embroidery thread taut in your right hand while twisting the necklace. Keep it layered nicely and tight (with no twine showing through) as you go.

9. Continue wrapping, pushing the wrap down toward the necklace occasionally to make sure the twine is well covered, until about 7½" (19cm) of the twine tails are covered.

10. Now, fold the twine ends back in toward the necklace so you have a loop approximately 1" (2.5cm) long, for the closure. Complete 2 half hitches here to secure the loop (E).

11. Continue wrapping over the closure loop until the opening is small enough to just fit over the button. Finish and secure with a clove hitch (see Appendix, page 186) over top of necklace closure (F). Cut the hemp ends and secure with a dab of glue.

12. Repeat this wrapping process on the other side until it matches the completed first side. Tie an overhand knot with thread and hemp ends. Pull tightly.

13. Using needle and thread, sew the button about ½" (13cm) in from the end of the strand. Trim ends and secure with a dab of glue.

COLOR-BLOCK SCARF

This long scarf takes any winter outfit to the next level, thanks to a lighter alpaca blend that creates a soft, floaty look. Add a fringe of super-fuzzy suri alpaca to the ends and you have a flirty bohemian yet sophisticated accessory. Experiment with different yarn weights and fibers to create a look that is uniquely you!

materials

240 yd (219.5m) of chunky-weight yarn (color A), (**5**), combining 2 x 20-yard (18.9m) lengths

100 yd (91.4m) of fuzzy worsted-weight yarn (color B), (**4**), combining 5 x 20-yard (18.9m) lengths

600 yd (548.6m) of chunky-weight yarn (color C), (**5**), combining 5 x 120-yard (109m) lengths

yarn used

2 skeins Blue Sky Alpaca Techno in Fame, 120 yd (109m), 1¾ oz (50g), 68% baby alpaca, 22% silk, 10% extra fine merino (color A)

1 skein Blue Sky Alpaca Brushed Suri in Whipped Cream, 142 yd (130m), 1¾ oz (50g), 67% baby suri alpaca, 22% merino, 11% bamboo (color B)

5 skeins Blue Sky Alpaca Techno in Metro Silver, 120 yd (109m), 1¾ oz (50g), 68% baby alpaca, 22% silk, 10% extra fine merino (color C)

sizes & measurements

Approximately 14" (35.5cm) wide, 96" (244cm) long

» Measurements will vary slightly based on your arm size, tension, and yarn choice.

yarn preparation

Measure five 20-yd (18.9m) strands of color A. Measure two 20-yd (18.9m) strands of color B. Combine and set aside these 7 strands for the first color-blocked section. Repeat this measurement and combination process so you have yarn set aside for the second color-blocked section. (See Arm-Knitting Yarn Preparation, page 182.)

1. Cast on 12 stitches to your right arm with colors A/B, holding all 7 strands together. Knit 5 rows. Trim the working yarn to approximately 8" (20.5cm). Reserve any excess yarn for making tassels later.

2. Change colors, switching the working yarn to 5 strands of color C (see page 170).

3. Continuing with color C, arm knit until the scarf measures approximately 80" (203cm) or your desired length, keeping in mind there is still a 16" (40.5cm) color-blocked section remaining. End with all of the stitches on your left arm.

4. Switch the working yarn back to colors A/B and knit 5 rows. Then bind off all 12 stitches.

5. For tassels, cut 16" (40.5cm) strands from any and all remaining yardage of color A and color B yarns. Distribute the strands evenly into 12 piles. Each pile should have 8–10 strands of yarn.

6. To make a tassel, fold one pile in half. Thread the folded end through the edge of the scarf (**A**), making a loop. Bring the loose ends through the loop (**B**). Pull each tassel taut and adjust each knot at the scarf's edge. Add 6 tassels spaced evenly to each end of the scarf.

7. Weave in all loose ends from the knitting and color changes.

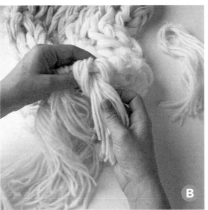

POM-POM HAT

Nothing exudes that fun, flirty, ready-for-adventure-at-the-drop-of-a-hat vibe like a giant pom-pom! Dropping this hat, however, will not be on your agenda. Flipping arm knitting to the purl side allows the big arm-knit stitches to stretch horizontally and form a warmer, tighter fabric. The modern horizontal stitches contrast beautifully with the cheery pom!

materials

162 yd (148m) of "slim" super-bulky yarn, (**6**), combining 6 x 27-yard (24.7m) lengths. The traditional knitting gauge for "slim" super-bulky is 2.75 sts per inch.

12" (30.5cm) twine or embroidery thread

5" x 4" (12.5cm x 10cm) piece of cardboard or other firm, rectangular object, for making the pom-pom

» See Yarn and Materials (pages 140–145) for an explanation of super-bulky yarns.

yarn used

2 skeins Purl Soho Super Soft Merino in Peacock Blue, 87 yd (79.5m), 3½ oz 100g), 100% Peruvian merino wool

sizes & measurements

9" (23cm) tall, with an adjustable circumference (see step 5)

» Measurements will vary slightly based on your arm size, tension, and yarn choice.

yarn preparation

Measure and cut six 27-yd (25m) strands of yarn. Combine these 6 strands to create the yarn for the project. (See Arm-Knitting Yarn Preparation, page 182.)

1. Cast on 9 stitches to your right arm. Knit 7 rows.

2. On the next row, knit 1 stitch, then knit 2 stitches together, creating a decrease (page 175). Repeat knit 1, knit 2 together until the end of the row. There are now 6 stitches on your arm.

3. Take the 6 stitches off your arm, and put them on 2 of your fingers. Starting at the stitch farthest from the working yarn, tighten each stitch taut across your fingers, lengthening the working yarn as you go (A).

4. Bring the working yarn through the 6 stitches, starting with the stitch farthest from the working yarn, creating a circle (B). Pull the working yarn tight.

5. Starting opposite the cast-on tail, stretch out the cast-on edge (the bottom stitches) evenly (C) such that it will fit around the circumference of your head when stretched. The width of the bottom of the hat when laid flat should be about 4" (10cm) less than the circumference of your head.

. . . .

Tip: Don't loosen the edge too much, as it is difficult to tighten it back up. If in doubt, leave the knitting tighter and adjust stitches after you've seamed the hat and tried it on. If it's pretty close in size, it will likely stretch enough to fit around your head. If you can't make it loose enough to fit your head, check first to see that you've loosened up the cast-on edge as much as possible. If you have and it still doesn't fit, you may need to reknit the hat with an extra stitch or add bulk to the yarn (see Troubleshooting Arm Knitting, page 184).

. . . .

6. Bring the side edges of the hat together, with the purl side facing out (D). Mattress stitch (page 181) the edges together, and then weave in the ends.

7. Make a pom-pom by wrapping the remaining length of yarn around a 5" x 4" (12.5cm x 10cm) piece of cardboard—or a smartphone! Pull the looped yarn off the rectangle, keeping the yarn wound in its shape (E).

8. Wrap a 12" (30.5cm) piece of twine around the center of the looped yarn (F). Tie a secure knot. Reknot, tying the center as tightly as possible. Then cut the loops of yarn (G).

9. Trim the pom-pom ends to shape the yarn into a ball, being careful not to trim the twine ties (H).

10. Attach the pom-pom to the top of the hat by threading the 2 twine ties through the yarn at the hat's center top (I). Tie the twine securely inside the hat.

TWO-TONE DOG COLLAR

This collar attracts attention like you wouldn't believe. No one can figure out how it's done, but now you can! As you'll quickly learn, the two-tone effect is created simply by weaving a second color through the finger knitting as you go. Find some cotton, nylon, or leather cording and, before you know it, your beloved pet will be wowing others with his or her own unique style.

PROJECT TYPE
finger knitting

SKILL LEVEL
intermediate

. . . .

TECHNIQUES
Casting on................... 151
Two-finger knitting 151
Binding off 151

materials

16' (4.9m) of natural 3mm 100% cotton cording (color A)

2' (61cm) of black 3mm 100% cotton cording (color B)

1" (2.5cm) quick-release buckle

materials used

Darice Craft Designer Macrame Cord, 3mm, in Natural, 100% cotton, (color A)

Darice Craft Designer Macrame Cord, 3mm, in Black, 100% cotton (color B)

sizes & measurements

1" (2.5cm) wide, up to 19" (48.5cm) in circumference

1. Leaving a 6" (15cm) tail, complete a two-finger cast-on with color A (white). Thread and fold color B (black) in half around the lower strand on your middle finger (A).

2. While keeping the folded strand of color B at the front of your hand, bring the lower strands over the top, completing 1 row with color A (B). Tighten the tail.

3. Bring the color B cord through your two fingers to the back (C). Work a row of stitches in A. Make sure, as you wrap, to bring the color A working cord over (not under) the color B cord at the back of your hand.

. . . .

Tip: "Working a row" includes wrapping the yarn and pulling the strands over the top.

. . . .

4. Bring the folded cord in color B to the front and work a row of stitches in color A.

. . . .

Tip: When working with a slippery material, use more effort to keep the knitting fairly tight as you go. After you pull a pair of stitches over, tighten the set of loops still on your fingers before you wrap a new set.

. . . .

5. Repeat steps 3 and 4 until your desired length. As you pass the folded color B cord back and forth (D), for the best visual effect, keep the strands parallel; do not twist them.

6. Pull the collar taut and measure the length against an existing collar or your pet's neck, making sure to incorporate the length of the buckle. Take note that the side facing your hand is the "right" side, while the other side is the "wrong" side. The right side will show more of the center cord.

7. Bind off, leaving at least 6"–8" (15cm–20.5cm) of cord remaining in both colors to attach the buckle ends. Pull collar taut before you cut. The folded center cord should be parallel the whole way through the collar.

8. Pull the buckle apart. Attach the male half of the buckle to the beginning of the collar (right side up) first. Bring the loop of the center folded cord (color B) through the opening in the buckle half and then up and over the buckle (E). Pull taut.

9. String the initial starting length of the cord (color A) through the buckle opening and around the finger-knit strand such that it makes a pattern of 2 loops on each side of the color B loops on the buckle (F).

10. Bring color A behind the buckle. Repeat step 9 and tighten, turning the attachment into a pretty design feature.

11. Pull the collar taut so that color A is stretched across the center cord (color B), not bunched up. Straighten the center cord again so it lies flat.

12. With the right side of the collar facing you, thread each strand of the center cord (color B) through the female side of the buckle (G), bringing the cord back around and across the front to reflect the pattern from the other buckle attachment. Next thread color A through the collar (H) and the buckle (I) twice, bringing the cord across the front to match the pattern of the other side.

13. Bring all loose cords from both ends to the back of the work, burying the cord in the wrong side of the collar. Trim ends.

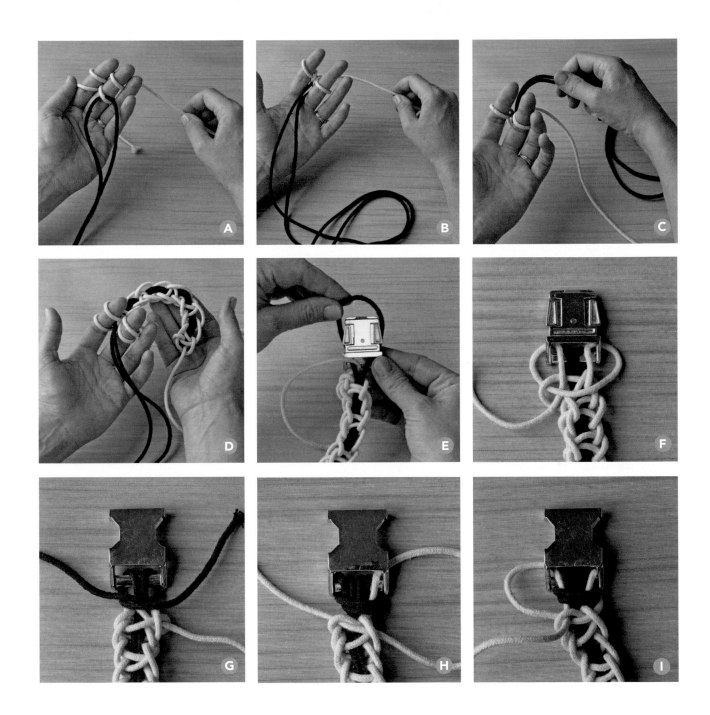

SLOUCH HAT

Tailgates in November winds, sleigh rides through the forest, or an outdoor New Year's Eve—adventures abound, and you can be warm and stylish through them all. This cozy hat will keep your rosy cheeks and cold nose in fashionable company. Mix two colors to create a fun variegated yarn that complements the laid-back slouch.

materials

129 yd (155.5m) of "slim" super-bulky yarn (color A), (**6**), combining 3 x 43-yard (39m) lengths. The traditional knitting gauge for "slim" super-bulky is 2.75 sts per inch.

86 yd (79m) of "slim" super-bulky yarn (color B), (**6**), combining 2 x 43-yard (39m) lengths. The traditional knitting gauge for "slim" super-bulky is 2.75 sts per inch.

» See pages 140–145 for an explanation of super-bulky yarns.

yarn used

2 skeins Purl Soho Super Soft Merino in Desert Blue, 87 yd (79.5m), 3½ oz (100g), 100% Peruvian merino wool (color A)

1 skein Purl Soho Super Soft Merino in Ice Blue, 87 yd (79.5m), 3½ oz (100g), 100% Peruvian merino wool (color B)

sizes & measurements

12" (30.5cm) long, with an adjustable circumference (see step 11)

» Measurements will vary slightly based on your arm size, tension, and yarn choice.

yarn preparation

Cut five 43-yd (39m) strands of yarn: 3 strands from color A and 2 strands from color B. Combine and hold those 5 strands to make the yarn for this project. (See Arm-Knitting Yarn Preparation, page 182). If you use the suggested yarn, 43 yd (39m) is approximately half the skein.

1. Cast on 16 stitches to your right arm.

2. Knit 7 rows.

3. On the next row, knit 2 stitches together, creating a decrease (page 175). Repeat this decrease across the entire row. There are now 8 stitches on your arm.

4. Take the 8 stitches off your arm. Starting at the stitch farthest from the working yarn, tighten each stitch taut across your fingers, lengthening the working yarn as you go (**A**).

5. Bring the working yarn through the 8 stitches, starting with the stitch farthest from the working yarn, creating a circle (**B**). Pull the working yarn tight.

6. Bring the sides of the hat together, with the knit side facing out (**C**). Leaving 1 yd (0.9m) of length to seam the hat, trim the working yarn. Reserve the remaining yarn for the hat band.

7. Sew the hat seam using mattress stitch (page 181). Tie a knot between the original tail and your working yarn and weave in the 2 ends (**D**).

8. Try on the hat, expanding the cast-on edge only enough for the hat to feel comfortably snug on your head.

9. To make the hat band, use the reserved 5-stranded yarn. Leave an 8" (20.5cm) tail and bring a loop of yarn from inside the hat up into the first stitch to the left of the seam (**E**).

10. Use a slip stitch (page 179) to chain around the edge of the hat (**F**). Make 1 chain stitch for every arm knit stitch in the hat (**G**); if you cast on 16 stitches, you will make

15 chains because you lose 1 stitch in the seam. You can manipulate the size of the chain stitch, making it tighter or looser as you go. Right now, try to make it even with the circumference of the hat that fit comfortably on your head.

11. After making 1 round with the slip stitch, try the hat on again. If it is too tight, you need to undo the slip-stitch chain and work it again a little looser. If the hat is too loose, you need to make the slip stitch smaller, bringing in the circumference of the overall hat.

12. Once you feel comfortable with the fit, begin another chain of slip stitch above the one you just made (**H**). Keep the slip stitch chain confined to the very first row of stitches on the hat.

13. When you come around to the beginning, try the hat on again. It should be comfortably snug on your head. Redo the last round of slip stitch if necessary for a good fit. Now begin the 3rd and final chain, with the slip stitches still pulled through the first row of stitches in the hat. If you need more room, push the other 2 chains toward the bottom of the hat as you go.

14. When you come around to the seam again, cut the working yarn, leaving an 8" (20.5cm) tail (**I**). Bring the tail up through the last chain and then to the back of the work.

15. Weave in this tail.

BEANIE HAT

Bring on the hustle and bustle of city streets. This warm beanie is a charming companion for the changing seasons. Simply switch the yarn color after two rows to create a "colorwork" pattern that only *looks* complex. This sophisticated topper is ready for downtown strolls and hours of window-shopping.

materials

45 yd (41m) of "slim" super-bulky yarn (color A), (🔟), combining 6 x 8-yard (7.5m) lengths. The traditional knitting gauge for "slim" super-bulky is 2.75 sts per inch.

72 yd (66m) of "slim" super-bulky yarn (color B), (🔟), combining 6 x 12-yard (11m) lengths. The traditional knitting gauge for "slim" super-bulky is 2.75 sts per inch.

» See pages 140–145 for an explanation of super-bulky yarns.

yarn used

1 skein Purl Soho Super Soft Merino in Peacock, 87 yd (79.5m), 3½ oz (100g), 100% Peruvian merino wool (color A)

1 skein Purl Soho Super Soft Merino in Sea Salt, 87 yd (79.5m), 3½ oz (100g), 100% Peruvian merino wool (color B)

sizes & measurements

9" (23cm) high, with an adjustable circumference (see step 7)

» Measurements will vary slightly based on arm size, tension, and yarn choice.

yarn preparation

Measure and cut six 12-yd (11m) strands of color B. Combine these 6 strands to create the yarn for the project. Set aside color B. Measure and cut six 8-yd (7.5m) strands of color A. Combine these 6 strands for color A yarn. (See Arm-Knitting Yarn Preparation, page 182).

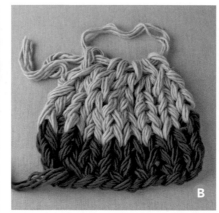

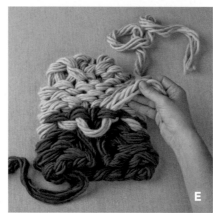

1. Cast on 9 stitches to your right arm with color A, holding all 6 strands together. Knit 2 rows.

2. Switch the working yarn to 6 strands of color B (see page 170), leaving a color A tail of approximately 10" (25.4cm).

3. Continuing with color B, knit 5 rows.

4. On the next row, knit 1 stitch, then knit 2 stitches together, creating a decrease (page 175). Repeat knit 1, knit 2 together to the end of the row. There are now 6 stitches on your arm.

5. Take the 6 stitches off your arm, and put them on 2 of your fingers. Starting at the stitch farthest from the working yarn, tighten each stitch taut across your fingers, lengthening the working yarn as you go (**A**).

6. Bring the working yarn through the 6 stitches, starting with the stitch farthest from the working yarn, creating a circle (**B**). Pull the working yarn tight.

7. Starting opposite the cast-on tail, stretch out the cast-on edge evenly such that it will fit around the circumference of your head when stretched (C). The width of the bottom of the hat when laid flat should be about 4" (10cm) less than the circumference of your head. Test for fit by stretching around your head.

. . . .

Tip: Don't loosen the edge too much, as it is difficult to tighten it back up. If in doubt, leave the knitting tighter and adjust stitches after you've seamed the hat and tried it on. If you can't make it loose enough to fit your head, you may need to reknit the hat with 1 extra stitch or add bulk to the yarn (see Troubleshooting Arm Knitting, page 184).

. . . .

8. Bring the side edges of the hat together with the purl side facing out. With the working yarn, mattress stitch (page 181) the edges of the first color section together (D).

9. When you reach the color change, unknot the yarn tails from the color switch. Bring the tail in color B over and through the purl stitch on the other side of the hat to make a faux stitch (E). Push that yarn through the knit fabric and leave on inside of hat. Bring the tails to the inside of the hat.

10. Next, using the tail (F), finish the mattress stitch seam with color A.

11. Weave in the ends. Weave both ends of color A through the edge of the hat (instead of the seam) to keep the seam from getting too bulky (see page 169).

CASHMERE SCARF

It's striped. It's sharp. It's just the thing for your favorite guy. In subtle hues of green, this savvy scarf will win every time. The soft cashmere's elegant drape keeps the scarf from being bulky or hot. The only problem is that you'll be dying to borrow it. Make sure to knit another for yourself!

materials

100 yd (91.4m) of worsted-weight yarn (color A), (4)

100 yd (91.4m) of worsted-weight yarn (color B), (4)

yarn used

1 skein Jade Sapphire 8-ply Cashmere in Sea Glass, 100 yd (91.4m), 1.9 oz (55g), 100% cashmere (color A)

1 skein Jade Sapphire 8-ply Cashmere in Malachite, 100 yd (91.4m), 1.9 oz (55g), 100% cashmere (color B)

sizes & measurements

5½" (14cm) wide, 66" (168cm) long

note

» The stripes are created by attaching a contrasting finger-knit strand to a finished strand. The finished strand will shrink in length as you attach the new strand to it, because the original curl of the strand flattens out as you use the outside stitches of the strand to knit. If exact length is important to you, create a swatch of 3 stripes and 15 rows. Measure the length of that swatch to calculate how many rows you need to knit to reach your desired length.

1. With color A, finger knit a four-finger strand for 116 rows, or to the desired length.

2. Bind off without pulling the working yarn tightly. The end should stay relatively uncurled, similar in width to the rest of the strand.

3. Turn the strand so that the purl side faces up with the start of the strand at the top (**A**).

4. Place the outermost and first stitch from the finished finger-knit strand onto your forefinger. With color B, wrap the yarn to start a finger-knit row (**B**).

5. Complete the row, pulling the bottom 2 wraps over the top when you get to your forefinger—a "forefinger join." One row is attached (**C**).

6. For the next row, pick up the next stitch from the finished strand and place it on your forefinger again (**D**).

7. Now, wrap the yarn to finger knit a row (**E**). Finger knit as usual, again pulling the 2 bottom strands on your forefinger over the top.

8. Continue finger knitting, matching the old strand to the new one row for row for 116 rows or until you reach the end. Bind off.

9. Repeat the length of attached finger knitting with color A, remembering to orient the completed knit strands purl side up, again beginning at the start of the strands.

10. Continue to attach strands in alternating colors until you have completed 5 stripes total, or to the desired width. Weave in all ends.

11. Next, with color B, you will create a border by completing a two-finger strand around the entire scarf and attaching it to the outermost stitches as you go. This strand is attached with the wrong side (or purl side) face up, the opposite direction of how you've been attaching the other strands to make the scarf. Orient the scarf right side up and begin at the lower right-hand corner.

12. With color B, along the short end of the scarf, complete a two-finger strand and forefinger join for approximately 12 evenly spaced rows. Collect 2 strands of yarn from the end of the scarf for each row (**F**). Don't worry about which exact strands to pick up; picking up 2 strands helps increase the stability of the border on the end. The border will curl over most of the edge. For each row, pull the bottom 3 strands (including the 2 you just picked up) over the top on your forefinger on each row. (**G**).

· ·

Tip: The neater the ends of your finger knitting (page 155), the neater the border will be across the end of the scarf.

· ·
· ·

Reverse Finger-Knit Border: Finger knitting on its own has a tendency to curl in at the sides. Adding a reverse border, which will curl in the opposite direction to the main fabric, helps flatten the overall piece. This border gives your piece a finished look, evening out the ends and edges. You can use this technique to create a finished edge around any of the attached finger-knitting techniques. This reverse border can be completed with either a two-finger (shown here) or a four-finger knit strand.

· ·

13. Turn the corner by finger knitting an extra row through the corner stitch.

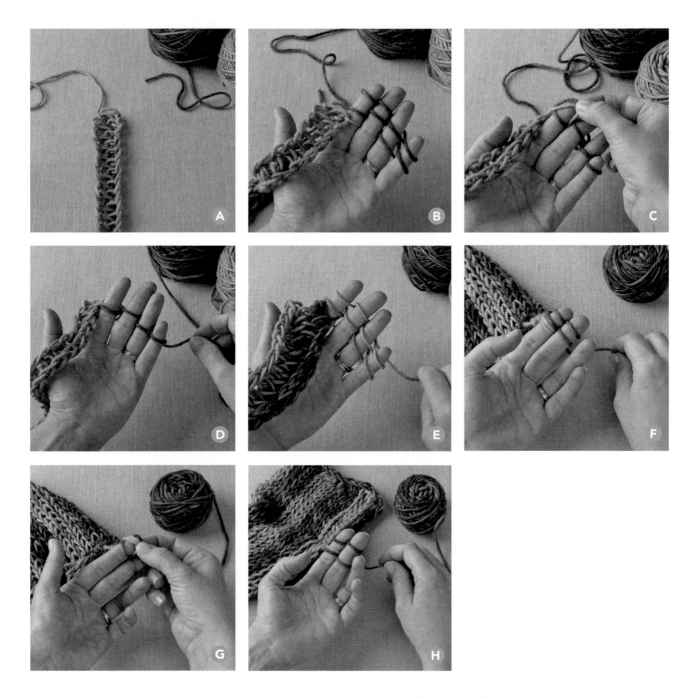

14. Along the sides, pick up only the outer-most strand of the outermost stitch with your forefinger (H) and continue finger knitting your border. At each corner, finger knit 2 rows.

15. When you get back to the other short end, remember to pick up 2 strands for each of approximately 12 rows.

16. The final row of finger knitting should include the first stitch of the first row of the border. Merge these strands by weaving the ends through the beginning and end of the border so the joining is as invisible as possible. Weave in all ends and block the scarf (page 157).

PURL-SIDE TOTE

I adore this oversized arm-knit tote. The scale of it feels graphic and modern, and the leather handles add just the right finish. Line it with a bright, fresh floral print and you'll have a bag that will make you happy every day!

materials

300 yd (274.5m) of "big" super-bulky yarn, (**6**), combining 4 x 75 yard (68.5m) lengths. The traditional knitting gauge for "big" super-bulky is 1.75–2.0 sts per inch. A lightweight jumbo yarn (**7**) (1.5 sts per inch) would also work well.

Butcher or tracing paper

1 yd (0.9m) internal liner fabric

1 yd (0.9m) external liner fabric (to match the yarn)

2½ yd (2.3m) fusible interfacing

Thread to match lining fabrics

12 solid brass plain Chicago bolts

72" (172cm) of 1" (2.5cm) wide leather strapping

» See pages 140–145 for an explanation of super-bulky yarns.

tools

Scissors, ruler, and pencil

Iron and ironing surface

Sewing machine, straight pins, sewing needle, and thread

Leather rotary punch, craft knife

yarn used

3 skeins Cascade Magnum in Camel, 123 yd (112.5 m), 8.82 oz (250 g) 100% wool

sizes & measurements

24" (61cm) wide, 19" (48.5cm) length

» Measurements will vary slightly based on your arm size, tension, and yarn choice.

» Easily cast on fewer stitches and knit fewer rows to achieve a smaller sized tote. The instructions are still the same, though required yardage will be less!

Combine and hold 4 strands together to create the yarn for this project. For large arm-knitting projects, it is easiest to knit directly from full skeins according to the number of strands recommended for the project (in this case, 4). Depending on the yardage available in each yarn skein, sometimes splitting skeins to achieve the overall desired length of yarn is a more cost-effective and efficient use of yarn. (See Arm-Knitting Yarn Preparation, page 182).

Knit the Shell

1. Cast on 12 stitches to your arm.

2. Knit for 30 rows.

3. When you initially cast on arm knitting, the cast-on edge is tighter than the stitches that follow. This tote gets its trapezoidal shape by leaving the cast-on stitches slightly tighter than the main fabric. Stretch out the cast-on edge to reach the desired width of bag top, and bind off the stitches at a tension to match that width. Do not cut the working yarn. Bring the yarn balls through the last loop.

4. Fold the piece in half with the short sides together and the purl side of the fabric facing out.

5. Beginning in the upper left-hand side of the bag and matching the sides stitch for stitch (**A**), use the working yarn to slip stitch the sides together (**B**) by completing the slip stitch through the outermost stitch on both sides of the bag (see Slip Stitch Finishing, page 179). Try to make the slip stitches match the size of each row.

6. Continue joining until you reach the fold in the bag. Make an extra slip stitch into the fold to allow the slip stitch to make the turn. Turn the bag over and continue to slip stitch up the other side of the seam, picking up the first stitch on the back side of the seam (just 1 loop) (**C**). Making the chained stitches appear on both sides of the bag is for appearance only.

7. At the top of the bag, slip stitch an extra chain into the corner stitch (**D**) to help make the turn and continue to slip stitch across one side of the top, making 1 slip stitch for each stitch of the row (**E**).

8. When you get to the other side of the bag, join these 2 sides together using a slip stitch as well, making an extra slip stitch in the corner. Slip stitch up the other side of the seam as in step 6.

9. When you get back to the top, make an extra slip stitch in the corner and then slip stitch across the other side of the top.

10. When you reach the place you started, trim the working yarn to 10" (25.5cm). Bring the end of the working yarn through the last chain you made and then feed that yarn back through the bag (**F**). Weave in all ends.

Sew the Lining

1. Place the tote on a piece of butcher paper or tracing paper. Organize the tote in the most symmetrical shape you can and trace around it (**G**).

2. Use a ruler to straighten out wiggly lines and make the shape consistent, so that the bottom corners are equidistant from the top corners.

3. Draw a dotted line 1" (2.5cm) inside the outline of the bag (**H**). This line represents the internal shape of the lining after construction.

4. Cut out your pattern piece along the solid outline of the bag. Fold the pattern piece under at the dotted lines, indicating the seam allowance, and determine whether the lining will fit in the bag well by placing the pattern piece inside the knit tote (**I**). Take special care

to make sure that the pattern piece extends across the full edge of the tote top.

5. Unfold the edges of the pattern piece. Fold the internal liner fabric (the one you'll see when you look in the bag) with the selvedges matching. Place the pattern piece; the bottom should be along the fold. Cut the fabric along the solid lines of the pattern piece.

6. Repeat step 5 with the external lining fabric (the one that will be visible in between the knit stitches).

7. Cut and apply a fusible interfacing to both the internal liner fabric and the external liner fabric, following the manufacturer's directions.

8. Place the right sides of the internal lining together. Sew a 1" (2.5cm) seam down both sides. Trim the seam to ⅛" (3mm) with sharp scissors.

9. Repeat step 8 with external lining fabric.

10. For both the internal and external liner, create the bottom of the bag by stitching a triangle shape at each corner. To do this, start with the bottom of the bag facing you and give a pull on the sides of the bag to make a

triangle shape at the corner; the side seam will run straight down the other side of your triangle. Sew a line across this triangle 1" (2.5cm) in from the point (J).

11. Turn the internal liner right side out and insert into the external liner so that the right sides of each liner are facing each other (K). Line up the seams at the center and then pin the liners together along the top.

12. Sew a 1" (2.5cm) seam along the top of the liners, leaving an 8" (20.5cm) opening in the center of one side to turn the liners inside out. Pull the interior and exterior liners out through the opening.

13. Arrange the internal liner inside the external liner, tucking the edges of the opening inside and pinning them together. Topstitch around the top of the liners at ½" (13mm).

14. Drop the liner into the knit shell, tucking it underneath the row of slip stitches along the top and making it an even distance from the top of the bag all the way around; pin the liner to the shell. With a needle and thread, sew the liner to the knit tote, following the lines and holes from your topstitching (L).

Add the Handles

1. Cut leather strapping to two 34" (86cm) pieces and four 1" (2.5cm) pieces.

2. With a leather rotary punch in a size to match your Chicago bolts, poke two holes in the end of one of the 34" (86cm) leather straps $5/8$" (16mm) and $1\,3/8$" (3.5cm) from the end.

3. Insert the nonscrew part of the bolts into the strap. Line the strap and bolts where you want them on the outside of the bag—the edge of my strap is placed 4" (10cm) in from the sides and 6" (15cm) down from the top. Holding the strap and fittings tightly against bag while ensuring that the lining is straight, reach inside the bag and feel for bolt indentations. Use a craft knife to poke a small hole through the lining fabric at the indentations into the screw hole of the bolts (M).

4. Bring screw sides of the bolts through the fabric lining holes (N), poking them through the yarn stitches as necessary. Match the strap piece to the screws and tighten down the bolts.

5. Repeat steps 2–4 for the other end of the same strap on the opposite side of the bag.

6. Repeat steps 2–5 to attach the second strap.

7. Once straps are in place, add another bolt where the straps cross the lip of the tote for extra stability. Punching a hole in the strap where necessary, sandwich the strap, knit bag lip, and a 1" (2.5cm) leather square placed on the inside of the tote to stabilize (O). Secure and tighten bolt.

CHAPTER 2

LIVE

Beautiful things happen when you combine the world of knitting without needles with that of home goods. Every piece in this chapter is modern, versatile, and uniquely designed to bring out the best in your personal style. Every piece is also shamelessly simple to make (but that can stay between us).

OVERSIZED PILLOWS

Lofty and luxurious—what a fabulous combination for a wow-worthy housewarming gift. Believe it or not, you can knit up one of these lavish pillows in just an evening. You'll quickly be tempted to knit up a few for your own relaxing retreat.

materials

26" x 26" (66cm x 66cm) pillow insert

¾ yd (68.5cm) of 54" (137cm) fabric

COLOR-BLOCKED PILLOW (LEFT):
240 yd (219.5m) of "big" super-bulky yarn, (6), for the color-blocked section, combining 4 x 30-yard (27.5m) lengths for each pillow side

492 yd (450m) of "big" super-bulky yarn, (6), for the main color, combining 4 x 61.5-yard (56.2m) lengths for each pillow side

MOSS STITCH PILLOW (RIGHT):
390 yd (357m) of "big" super-bulky weight yarn, (6), combining 3 x 130-yard (118.9m) lengths

The traditional knitting gauge for "big" super-bulky is 1.75–2.0 sts per inch. A lightweight jumbo yarn (7) (1.5 sts per inch) would also work well.

» See pages 140–145 for an explanation of super-bulky yarns.

tools

Ruler, fabric scissors, sewing needle or sewing machine, matching sewing thread

yarn used

COLOR-BLOCKED PILLOW (LEFT):
3 skeins Cascade Magnum in Ecru, 123 yd (112.5 m), 8.82 oz (250g), 100% wool (color A)

1 skein Cascade Magnum in Magenta, 123 yd (112.5 m), 8.82 oz (250g), 100% wool (color B)

MOSS STITCH PILLOW (RIGHT):
9 skeins Blue Sky Alpaca Bulky in Polar Bear (45 yd [41m]/ 3½ oz [100g]) 50% alpaca/ 50% wool

sizes & measurements

26" x 26" (66cm x 66cm)

yarn preparation

For the Color-Blocked Pillow, combine and hold together 4 strands to make the yarn. For the Moss Stitch Pillow, combine and hold together 3 strands to make the yarn. Try any of these patterns holding one strand more or less to get a knit fabric you're happy with. (See Arm-Knitting Yarn Preparation, page 182.)

notes on gauge:

» Because you are working on a piece that needs to fit an exact size, knit a gauge swatch before diving into the project. A gauge swatch helps you get the correct size if your arm size or if the way you knit is different than mine, or if you want to use a different yarn, stitch pattern, or pillow size.

Make a Gauge Swatch

1. Cast on 10 stitches. Knit 10 rows.

2. Using a ruler, measure how many stitches you get across a 10" (25.5cm) width. Try to be exact to ¼" (6mm). Divide that number by 10 to get the number of stitches per inch.

3. Next, multiply the number of stitches per inch by the number of inches you want in width; round up if necessary. That will give you the number of stitches to cast on.

Cover the Pillow

1. Pin together two 27" x 27" (68.5cm x 68.5cm) squares of fabric with right sides facing each other. Sew a ½" (13mm) seam around the entire perimeter, leaving a 10" (25.5cm) opening on one side.

2. Trim the seam to ¼" (6mm) and clip corners to remove extra fabric bulk. Turn inside out through the opening.

3. Insert the pillow form, tuck ½" (13mm) of the raw edges of the opening in, and sew closed.

Color-Blocked Pillow

1. With color A, cast on 15 stitches (or number indicated by gauge swatch) to your right arm.

2. Knit 15 rows.

3. Change to color B, leaving a long 4 yd (3.7m) tail of color A.

4. Knit 6 more rows in color B.

5. Bind off all stitches. Leave a long 2-yd (1.8m) tail of color B.

6. Repeat steps 1–5 for the other side of the pillow cover, but for this side, the cast-on tail and the bound-off tail can both be cut as short as 8" (20.5cm).

7. Weave the "short" ends into the second pillow cover piece.

8. Next, use the long color A tail to join the color A sections from the 2 pillow cover pieces. Line up the pillow sides, stitch for stitch, with right sides facing up. Use mattress stitch (page 181) to sew down one side (**A**), across the bottom (**B**), and up the other side. Weave the tail of color A into the seam you've just made.

9. Use the tail of color B to mattress stitch the color B sections. To do so, seam the 2 sides together down the short side of the color B section. Feed the tail back up to the top along the inside of the seam.

10. Insert the pillow into the pillow cover. Continue to mattress stitch along the top of the cover and down the other side of the color B section.

11. Secure the color B tail with a knot and tuck in the end along the side seam.

Moss Stitch Pillow

1. Cast on 14 stitches (or number indicated by gauge swatch) to your right arm.

2. Knit 1 stitch, and then purl 1 stitch (page 172). Repeat, alternating knit and purl stitches across the entire row.

3. Repeat step 2 until the piece measures 40 rows in total.

4. Bind off all stitches while continuing to complete the knit 1, purl 1 pattern. Leave a long 4-yd (3.7m) tail.

5. Fold the pillow cover in half, matching the corners. Using mattress stitch (page 181) and the long tail, seam down one side of the pillow.

6. Feed the yarn back up the seam, and use mattress stitch to seam across the top of the pillow cover.

7. Insert the pillow, and then mattress stitch down the other side (C). Weave in ends.

ROPE RUG

Using rope lends a hip industrial flair to a simple area rug. Tuck this large-scale piece under your favorite reading chair, let it stimulate your weary feet at the sink, or have it welcome guests at the front door. Any way you look at it, this is one rug you'll want to play footsie with.

materials

500 yd (457m) of 100% cotton rope, ¼" (6mm) in diameter

Electrical tape or glue (Fray Block dries quickly and clearly)

sizes & measurements

32" (81cm) wide, 42" (106.5cm) long

» Measurements will vary slightly based on arm size, tension, and rope choice.

yarn preparation

Combine and hold 3 strands of the rope together for this project. If you order the rope from a company like Knot & Rope Supply (page 188), you can ask for it to be cut into three 166.7-yd (152.5m) lengths in advance. Note that many rope suppliers measure in feet, not yards, so make sure you order enough!

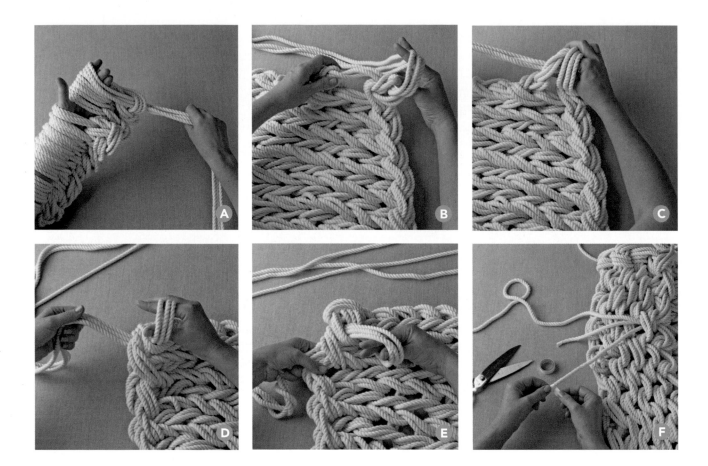

1. Cast on 18 stitches to your right arm. It will be a tight fit, so scoot the beginning stitches way up toward your elbow.

2. Knit 24 rows or to the desired finished length. Make the rug look more uniform by keeping the strands untwisted and consistently falling the same way with every stitch. Also, you may find it easier to knit the last few stitches on your hand instead of all the way on your arm (**A**). If you do so, try to keep the stitches a consistent size.

3. Bind off the stitches, pulling the rope all the way through the last stitch (**B**). You need approximately 19 yd (17.4m) of rope remaining to make the border.

Tip: Because of the nature of the material, the number of stitches, and the irregularity of using an arm as a needle, you will have some inconsistent stitches. You can move some of these around by pulling any extra length to the sides of the rug or by making some of the stitches more even across the work.

4. You will be making a border using a slip stitch finishing technique (page 179) around 3 sides of the rug. (You don't need to do the bound-off edge, which you just finished.) Starting at the lower right-hand side of the rug (B), complete a slip stitch by pulling a loop of yarn through the center of the outermost stitch. Reach into the loop you just made and pull the working yarn through it (C). Continue pulling the working yarn through the next stitch on the next row of the rug and then pulling it through the loop you just made. Pay attention to the strands of rope to keep them lying consistently.

5. When you get to the corner of the rug, make an extra stitch in the corner by making an extra chain (D).

6. When you get to the cast-on edge of the rug, bring your slip stitch through the space between each cast-on stitch (E).

7. Continue to the other long side of the rug. When you get back to the bound-off edge, pull the working yarn all the way through the last loop. Cut and weave in the ends. Wrap white electrical tape around the ends (F) or apply a clear glue (like Fray Block) to keep the rope from unraveling.

COVERED STOOL

I love rustic old stools. Every chip in the paint, crack in the wood, and wobble tells a story. Unearth one at a garage sale, in the back corner of an antiques shop, or even in your mother's attic. A hand-knit cover will make that treasure even more inviting. It deserves its own spot, right by the fireplace.

materials

80 yd (73m) of worsted-weight yarn, (**4**), for a stool top with an 11¼" [28.5cm] diameter

tools

Large safety pin

Scissors

Darning needle

Clip, such as a clothespin or binder clip

yarn used

1 skein Cascade Yarns Eco Duo in Vanilla, 200 yd (180m), 3½ oz (100g), 70% baby alpaca, 30% merino wool

» One 200-yd (180m) skein will make a cover for a stool up to 17" (43cm) in diameter.

sizes & measurements

Adjustable

note

» The stool in the photo is 11¼" (28.5cm) in diameter and 2" (5cm) deep. The small stool shown in step-by-step photos (page 71) measures 9" (23cm) in diameter and required approximately 50 yd (45.5m) of worsted-weight yarn.

» To knit the cover as one piece, try the attached spiral finger knitting as described in the Linen Baskets (page 89).

1. Cut 4 strands of yarn long enough to wrap across the diameter of the stool and tie underneath. These will be referred to as the "wrapping ties."

2. Finger knit a four-finger strand to the desired length. Don't bind off yet; place the stitches on a safety pin so you can continue knitting if needed after securing the strands to the stool.

Tip: Test the length as you go, following step 3, but don't forget to add enough length to cover the depth of the stool as well.

3. Weave in the tail yarn at the beginning of the strand. Place the strand in the center of the stool top and turn the end in a spiral, overlapping strands as you go (**A**). Work to keep the line of finger knitting untwisted as you spiral. It helps to pick a line of stitches within the finger-knit strand and keep it oriented toward the top. Spiral the strand until it covers the entire top of the stool.

4. Thread one of the wrapping ties on a darning needle. Run it straight through the spiral of finger knitting (**B**). It helps to go halfway across the spiral (**C**), pull the yarn through, and straighten the strands; then, thread the yarn through the second half (**D**) and straighten the strands. The tie should be buried within the finger-knit strands so that you don't see it. Adjust the wrapping tie so the excess length at both ends is equal.

Tip: Try to go through the finger-knit strands without splitting the strands of the yarn itself.

5. Thread the next wrapping tie through the spiral at a line perpendicular to the wrapping tie you just threaded, as though you were cutting a pie into 4 pieces. Next, go in between the 2 wrapping ties already in the stool top with the third piece of yarn. Finally, take the last one through the spiral where the biggest gap is, as though cutting a pie into eighths (**E**).

6. Carefully place the spiral on a flat work surface, with the right side facedown. Straighten the strands so they lie nicely. Place the stool upside down on top of the spiral; the edge of the stool should line up with the edge of the spiral.

7. Continue to bring the finger-knit strand around the stool edge, threading each wrapping tie through the back of the strand as you come to them (**F**). To cover the sides of the stool, the finger-knit strand needs a fair amount of tension and be snug on the stool as it goes around so it doesn't sag when you turn it over.

8. As you go, occasionally pull all the wrapping ties together and hold with a clip (**G**) and flip the stool over to make sure the sides will sit how you like; correct as necessary. Continue this process until you have covered the sides as desired, knitting more if needed (**H**).

9. Cut the strand 1" (5cm) away from the last wrapping tie (Cutting a Finger-Knit Strand, page 154), finish, and bind off. Secure strand to the stool by weaving in its end and knotting it to the finger-knit spiral.

10. Turn the stool upside down again and bring the ends of each individual wrapping tie

across the stool bottom and tie in a knot (I).
Turn the stool right side up one more time to
make sure it all fits as you would like. Trim the
wrapping ties and weave them in underneath
themselves so they don't hang down.

GIANT MONOGRAM

Make your space your own with a striking wall hanging. Using a variegated fiber adds extra interest and depth, while the modern font keeps it fresh. Using old cardboard and piles of finger knitting opens up all sorts of possibilities—imagine a fuzzy bunny in the nursery, a neon peace sign in your tween's room, or a frame around your son's favorite painting. Go dimensional and wrap a Styrofoam wreath, egg, or cone for dazzling holiday decor.

materials

450 yd (411.5m) of worsted-weight yarn, (**4**)

24" x 24" (61cm x 61cm) square of cardboard

Paper

Tape

Popsicle sticks (optional)

tools

Scissors

Craft knife

Small nails, pushpins, or hooks, for hanging the monogram

yarn used

5 skeins Madelinetosh ASAP in Vintage Sari, 90 yd (82m), 4½ oz (127g), 100% superwash merino wool

sizes & measurements

22" (56cm) wide, 22" (56cm) tall

1. Print your desired letter at a local print shop in a simple, bold font at a large-scale size. The monogram shown is 22" x 22" (56cm x 56cm), using the font Urban Grotesk. If desired, freehand the letter on cardboard, or use computer software, like Adobe Illustrator, to tile and print at home on 8½" x 11" (21.5cm x 28cm) paper.

2. Finger knit at least 30 yd (27.5m) of a four-finger knit strand and bind off.

3. Cut out the letter template with scissors and tape it to a piece of cardboard (**A**). Rotate the template a little so that the horizontal and vertical lines of the letter don't line up exactly with the corrugation. (For stability, it is better if you cross the corrugated parts of the cardboard at an angle.)

4. Using a craft knife, cut around the template through the cardboard to create the letter shape (**B**). If desired, reinforce pressure points (i.e., the down stroke in the bottom right-hand section of this a) with taped or glued-on popsicle sticks, especially if the letter will be resting on that piece.

5. To begin, wrap the strand of finger knitting around the bottom of the cardboard letter, overlapping the end of the strand in the back as you go (**C**). Straighten and untwist the finger-knit strand as you wrap. The strands should lie neatly side by side (D).

6. When you get to a part of the letter that has one line blending into another, alternate between angling the finger-knit strand into the new line of the letter and then around the old line of the letter (E). When you angle the strand into the new part of the letter from the old part, you will need to pull the length of strand under the wrap you just made (F). Repeat this process, condensing the strands as needed, until the blank space where the two lines of the letter join fills in. Then, continue to wrap around the straight parts of the letter.

7. If you get to the end of the strand, tuck it underneath the wrapped strands in the back, maintaining firm tension in the last couple of wraps around the letter. Start any new strands as in step 5.

8. When the letter is completely wrapped, cut the end of the finger-knit strand and rebind it off (page 154), leaving length to weave in the finger-knit strand end in the back.

9. Hang your letter! You can use small nails, pushpins, or hooks at the critical balance points in the letter's open places and underneath the letter. If you've wrapped

tautly enough, you can hook the wrapped strands from the back of the letter on a few large picture hooks. Or, if you open up a space between the strands on the face of the letter, you can drive small nails directly through the cardboard, and then realign the finger-knit strand over the nail. Secure both the top of the letter and the bottom so it sits flush against the wall.

GRAND POUF

Walking into a room with a sumptuous knitted pouf feels like a hearty greeting from the warmest of welcoming committees. Make a bunch for the kids to roll around on in front of the TV, or save it for your own quiet Saturday afternoon tea.

PROJECT TYPE
arm knitting

SKILL LEVEL
intermediate

. . . .

TECHNIQUES

Adjusting yarn gauge ..184

Casting on....................162

Arm knitting.................164

Purling 172

Binding off 168

Mattress stitch 181

materials

250 yd (229m) of large-scale jumbo yarn, (**7**), combining 2 x 125-yard (114m) lengths.

The traditional knitting gauge for this specialty jumbo yarn is 1 st per inch.

Stuffing (see Notes)

» See pages 140–145 for an explanation of weights and gauges.

» Replace this yarn with 4 strands of a lightweight jumbo yarn or 6 strands of a "big" super-bulky yarn held together.

yarn used

2 skeins Big Stitch Alpaca in Cream, 140 yd (128m), 40 oz (1,133g), 70% alpaca, 15% wool, 15% nylon

sizes & measurements

25" (63.5cm) wide, 16" (40.5cm) tall, 78" (198cm) circumference

Before seaming, the knitted piece measures approximately 25" (63.5cm) wide and 44" (112cm) long.

» Measurements will vary slightly based on arm size, tension, and yarn choice.

yarn preparation

Combine and hold 2 strands together for this project.

notes

An inexpensive king-size alternative-down comforter works great as stuffing; you also can use recycled plastic bags, T-shirts, or sheets. The closer the stuffing is to the yarn color, the less likely you will be able to see through the stitches. You can also make a drawstring sack or buy a laundry bag in the color of your yarn for holding the stuffing.

1. Cast on 12 stitches to your right arm, leaving 1 yd (0.9cm) of tail.

2. Knit 1 row.

3. Purl (page 172) the next row.

4. Repeat steps 2 and 3 for 34 rows, or until the piece measures 44" (112cm), ending with the stitches on your left arm.

5. Bind off all stitches, purling the stitches from this arm as you do so. Leave 1 yd (0.9m) of length for seaming. Make sure there are at least 4 additional yards (2.7m) remaining to finish the pouf.

6. Fold the piece, matching the short ends and lining the edges up stitch for stitch, with the tails at the bottom toward you and the bound-off edge on the left. Use the remaining yarn to seam the ends together with mattress stitch (page 181). Weave in both ends.

7. Thread a 1-yd (0.9m) length of yarn through the loop of every other end stitch along the entire side of your knitted fabric (**A**). It should look like you're closing a drawstring bag, but don't pull it tight yet!

8. Thread another 1-yd (0.9m) length of yarn through every end stitch that you didn't

collect the first time around. Draw the first round together as tightly as you can and knot the ends (B). Trim the yarn lengths no shorter than 8" (20.5cm) and pull them to the inside of the pouf.

9. Now, tighten the outer ring from step 7 like a drawstring bag (C), knot the yarn, and push it inside the shell.

10. Fill the pouf with stuffing (D).

11. Cut a new 1-yd (0.9m) length of yarn.

Repeat the gathering process on this end, collecting every other end stitch and knot the ends (E).

12. Go around again with a new length of yarn, threading it through each end stitch you didn't collect the first time. Draw the strands as tightly as you can (F). Knot the ends together. Trim all ends no shorter than 8" (20.5cm) and tuck them inside the pouf.

LACE PILLOWS

Structured but soft. Graphic but romantic. This lattice-work pattern is contradictory in the loveliest of ways. Despite the intricate look, the lace knits up in a snap! Matching the linen fabric to the yarn adds depth, but don't be afraid to stray from tone on tone. Try a sweet, small-scale vintage floral for a garden-inspired design.

PROJECT TYPE
arm knitting

SKILL LEVEL
advanced

. . . .

TECHNIQUES

Adjusting yarn gauge ..184

Casting on 162

Arm knitting 164

Increasing (yarn over)... 174

Decreasing (knit 2
    together) 175

Purling 172

Binding off 168

Weaving in ends 169

Blocking 181

materials

20" x 20" (51cm x 51cm) pillow form

162 yd (150m) of "slim" super-bulky yarn, (6), combining 6 x 27-yard (25m) lengths. The traditional knitting gauge for "slim" super-bulky is 2.75 sts per inch.

⅝ yd (57cm) of complementary fabric, at least 42" (106.5cm) wide

Thread to match the yarn

» See pages 140–145 for an explanation of super-bulky yarns.

tools

Fabric scissors

Sewing needle or sewing machine, and straight pins

yarn used

2 skeins each Purl Soho Super Soft Merino in Ballet Slipper, Oyster Gray, or Storm Gray, 87 yd (79.5m), 3½ oz (100g), 100% wool

fabric used

⅝ yd (57cm) Rowan Shot Cotton in Shell, or

⅝ yd (57cm) Robert Kaufman Essex in Grey or Steel

sizes & measurements

20" x 20" (51cm x 51cm), after blocking

yarn preparation

» Measure and cut six 27-yd (25m) strands. Combine and hold together these 6 strands to create the yarn for the project. (See Arm-Knitting Yarn Preparation, page 182.)

» If substituting a heavier super-bulky yarn, or if your knit cover ends up larger than desired, use fewer strands (4 or 5), and subsequently less yardage, for the project.

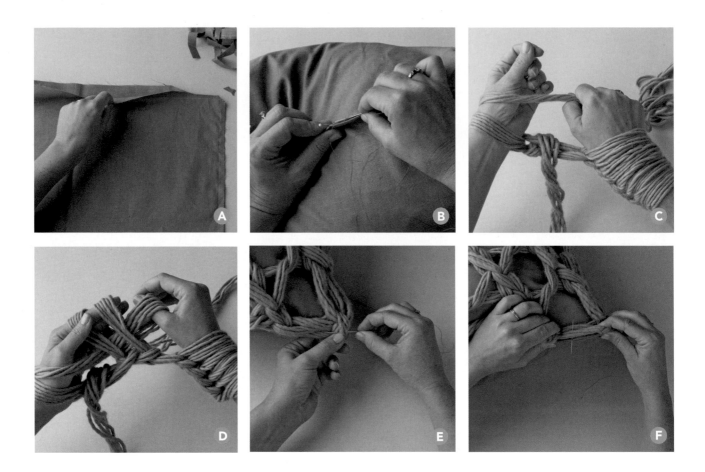

Cover the Pillow

· ·

Tip: If you find a pillow in a shade and fabric you like, skip making the cover.

· ·

1. Cut two 21" x 21" (53.3cm x 53.3cm) squares of fabric. Pin them together with right sides facing each other.

2. Sew a ½" (13mm) seam around all edges, leaving a 10" (25.5cm) opening in the middle of one side to insert the pillow form. Trim edges to ¼" (6mm) and snip off corners close to stitches to remove excess bulk (**A**).

3. Turn the pillow covering right side out and insert the pillow form into the cover. Turn the ½" (13mm) raw edges into the opening, pin, and stitch closed by hand (**B**), using the blind stitch (see Appendix, page 187).

Lace Front

1. Cast on 9 stitches to your right arm.

2. Knit 1 stitch. *Bring the yarn behind your left hand and let it rest over your left arm (**C**), creating an extra open stitch known as a yarn over. Knit the next 2 stitches together, creating a decrease (**D**). Repeat from * to the end of the row. At the end of the row, you should still have 9 stitches on your arm. Double-check to make sure you haven't accidentally dropped or added a stitch.

3. Purl 1 row (page 172).

4. Knit 2 stitches. *Bring the yarn behind your left hand and over your left arm (a yarn over). Knit 2 stitches together. Repeat from * to the last stitch; knit 1 stitch.

. . . .

Tip: Note that the pattern of stitches in step 4 is shifted 1 stitch from that in step 2.

. . . .

5. Purl 1 row.

6. Repeat steps 2–5 twice more, but on the very last purl row, bind off those stitches as you purl. Weave in ends.

7. Block your lace piece to 20" x 20" (51cm x 51cm) (page 178).

8. Pin the lace piece to the top of the pillow, matching the corners.

9. With needle and thread, stitch the corners of the lace piece to the face of the pillow (E), and then tack down the sides of the cover along the seams (F).

FAUX SHEEPSKIN

What a fabulous way to add texture to any nook! Create a luxe dining environment or a deliriously happy place to bury your feet in when you wake. Even transform a staid office chair into your favorite spot in the house with this fuzzy, sheep-friendly version of a boho-modern design staple.

materials

300 yd (274.5m) of "big" super-bulky yarn, (6), combining 3 x 100-yard (91.4m) lengths. The traditional knitting gauge for "big" super-bulky is 1.75–2.0 stitches per inch. A lightweight jumbo yarn (7) (1.5 sts per inch) would also work well.

568 yd (519m) of "fuzzy" worsted-weight yarn, (4), combining 4 x 142-yard (130m) lengths.

» See pages 140–145 for an explanation of super-bulky yarns.

yarn used

3 skeins Cascade Magnum in Cream, 123 yd (112.5m), 8.82 oz (250g), 100% Peruvian Highland wool

4 skeins Blue Sky Alpaca Brushed Suri in Whipped Cream, 142 yd (130m), 1¾ oz (50g), 67% baby suri alpaca, 22% merino, 11% bamboo

sizes & measurements

25" (63.5cm) wide, 34" (86cm) long

» Measurements will vary slightly based on arm size, tension, and yarn choice.

yarn preparation

Combine and hold together 3 strands of super-bulky yarn to create the yarn for the main body of this project. (See Arm-Knitting Yarn Preparation, page 182.)

When you reach step 14, combine and hold together 4 strands of the fuzzy worsted yarn to create the wooly loops.

1. Using the super-bulky yarn, cast on 15 stitches to your right arm.

2. Knit 4 rows.

3. Decrease 2 stitches on the next row by knitting the first 2 stitches and the last 2 stitches of the row together (see page 175). You will have 13 stitches on your arm.

4. Decrease 2 stitches on the next row in the same manner so that you have 11 stitches on your arm.

5. Knit 1 row.

6. Increase a stitch (see page 174) at the beginning of the next row by bringing the working yarn through the leg of the stitch in the row immediately below the current row (**A**). Repeat this increase at the end of the row (**B**), again by bringing the working yarn through the leg of the stitch in the row immediately below the current row (**C**). You will now have 13 stitches on your arm.

7. Increase 2 stitches on the next row at the beginning and end in the same manner for a total of 15 stitches.

8. Knit 4 rows.

9. On the next row, decrease 2 stitches, 1 at the beginning and 1 at the end of the row, reducing your stitch count by 2.

10. Repeat step 9; 11 stitches remain.

11. Knit 2 rows.

12. Repeat step 9 on the next three rows; 5 stitches remain.

13. Bind off all stitches. Trim and weave in all ends. The piece should be in the form of a sheepskin rug, with a couple of bulges along the edges and narrowing at the top (**D**).

14. To make the fuzzy surface, hold together 4 strands of the fuzzy worsted-weight wool. Make loops and tie knots for each individual stitch in the piece in the following manner:

» **Row 1:** Tie knots through the knit stitches. To go through each knit stitch, lay the length of yarn across the stitch (**E**), reach from underneath the stitch and pull one 3" (7.5cm) loop up under the first leg of the stitch and one 3" (7.5cm) loop through the other leg of the stitch (**F**). Tie these two loops in a knot (**G**). Repeat this process for each stitch in the entire row.

» **Row 2:** Tie knots straddling the knit stitches. To do this, lay the strand across the leg from 1 stitch and the leg from the adjacent stitch (**H**), bring 3" (7.5cm) loops underneath the leg from 1 stitch and the leg from the adjacent stitch (**I**), and knot those loops. In this method, at the beginning and end of the row, you will tie your loops around only one leg of the very first stitch and one leg of the very last stitch.

. . . .

Tip: Alternate which method you use to tie loops by row to avoid regularity in the piece. If you only tie the loops one way, they'll create grid-like lines up the piece.

. . . .

15. Repeat step 14 until you reach the end of the piece. Weave in all ends.

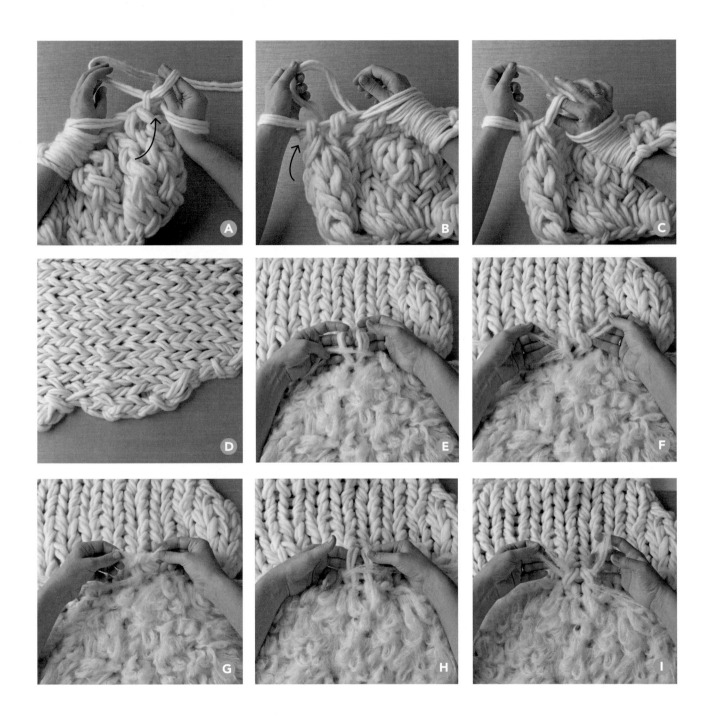

LINEN BASKETS

This technique uses the same concept as crochet in the round but with the look of knitting—I'm in love! Flip your basket inside out to create a different texture entirely. Now all you have to do is find something fun to put in them.

materials

LARGER BASKET: 540 yd (494m) of sportweight linen yarn, (3), combining 6 x 90-yard (82m) lengths

SMALLER BASKET: 252 yd (230.4m) of sportweight linen yarn, (3), combining 6 x 42-yard (38.4m) lengths

Scrap yarn in contrasting color

yarn used

3 skeins Louet Euroflax in Pewter, 270 yd (247m), 3½ oz (100g), 100% wet spun linen (makes both baskets)

sizes & measurements

LARGER BASKET: 8" (20.5cm) in diameter, 4" (10cm) tall

SMALLER BASKET: 6" (15cm) in diameter, 3¼" (8.5cm) tall

yarn preparation

To create the yarn for this basket, I used 6 strands of the sportweight. You want a yarn with some structure and stiffness to hold the shape of the basket; 2 strands of 2mm hemp cord also work well. (See Arm-Knitting Yarn Preparation, page 182, for strategies on splitting skeins.)

technique overview

» To make the finger-knit fabric for this basket, you spiral the finger knitting around, attaching it back to itself as you go, rather like crocheting in the round. As your circle expands, you need to add additional rows of finger knitting that aren't attached to add to the width of the circle. Once you reach your desired base size, you simply stop increasing, and your basket will start to develop sides.

1. Cut eight 3" (7.5cm) guide ties from scrap yarn and tie them to the working yarn, loose enough to slide up and down to help keep track of where you are in the spiral pattern (A).

2. Cast on and finger knit 3 rows of a two-finger knit strand (B).

3. Keeping the strand flat, twist it around so that you pick up the outside leg of the first stitch of the strand onto your forefinger (look for the loop with the tail coming out of it) (C). Wrap the yarn as you usually would, but on your forefinger pull the bottom 2 strands over the top strand (D).

4. Next, knit 1 row of regular finger knitting. (In this pattern, a "regular" row is also called an "unattached" row because you aren't linking it back to the circle). The unattached rows increase your circle size. Spiral the strand toward your forefinger, and finger knit an attached row by picking up the outside leg of the next available stitch in the spiral on your forefinger. (In the beginning, you will have to spiral farther than you think to reach the next loop.) Repeat 1 unattached row and 1 attached row twice more until you get back to the beginning (E), creating the initial circle.

5. Work 1 row unattached, bringing a tie up to the strand that you wrap around your middle finger (F). This marks the beginning of the round. *Attach 1 row by picking up the next available stitch in the spiral row (G) and work the row. Knit 1 row unattached. Repeat from * until the first guide tie.

Tip: This pattern is a general guideline to making the circle increase at a gradual rate. If your increases aren't exact or you don't end a round exactly at the spot of the tie, don't worry about it. As you pass the tie, simply start the next round as soon as you finish a set of the stitches from the prior round.

If the middle of the basket starts to bulge, it means that enough stitches weren't added somewhere along the way to keep the circle flat. If the base starts to ripple around the edge, likely too many stitches have been added. Pull out a round or two and play with the increase rate to make a flat circle.

6. Bring a guide tie up around your middle finger to indicate the start of a new round (H), as you *knit 1 row unattached. Knit 2 attached rows. Repeat from * until you reach the guide tie.

7. Bring another guide tie up and *knit 1 row unattached, knit 3 attached rows. Repeat from * around the circle until you reach the guide tie.

8. Bring another guide tie up and *knit 1 row unattached, knit 4 attached rows. Repeat from * until you reach the guide tie (I). For the small basket, stop after this round and skip to step 9. For the larger basket, keep going another 4 rounds, increasing the number of attached rows by 1 for each subsequent round.

Tip: If you've been marking each time you come around, the number of ties in the work also indicates the number of attached rows to complete in the pattern for that round.

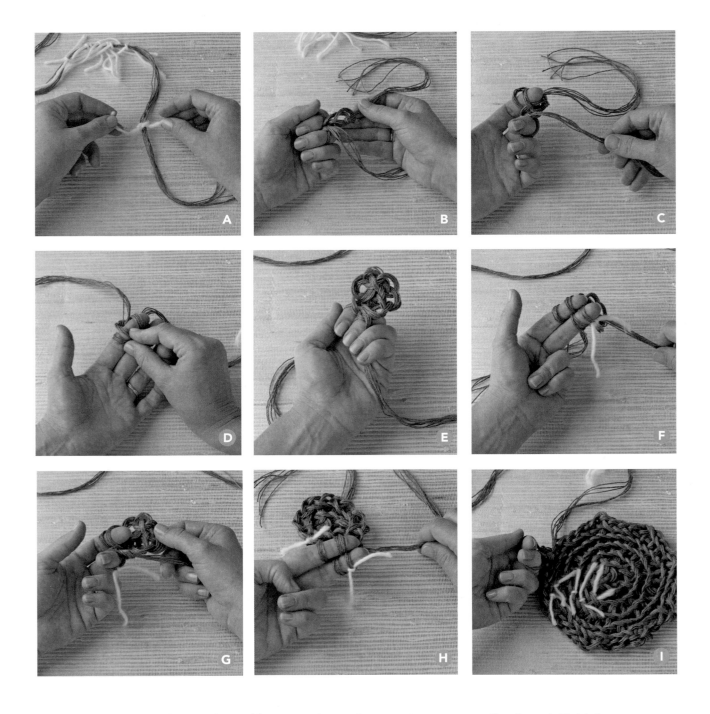

9. Once you reach your desired base size, knit attached rows only; the basket sides will start to curve. Make sure as the sides turn that you continue to pick up the outside leg of the stitch you just made. When you get to your desired basket height, end the round where your ties are generally aligned. Finish by binding off the finger-knit strand and weaving the ends into the basket.

10. Weave in the initial tail into the bottom of the basket.

CABLED BLANKET

The idea that you can make this gorgeous cable-knit blanket with just your arms and a pile of yarn still makes me giggle. Cables are an easy, traditional pattern, but the large scale is disarmingly modern. How chic would this look as a throw on your sofa, or charming spread over your daughter's bed?

materials

1,080 yd (987m) of "big" super-bulky yarn, (**6**), combining 3 x 360-yard (329m) lengths. The traditional knitting gauge for "big" super-bulky is 1.75–2.0 sts per inch. A lightweight jumbo yarn (**7**) (1.5 sts per inch) would also work well.

Scrap yarn in contrasting color or wrapping-paper tube

» See pages 140–145 for an explanation of super-bulky yarns.

yarn used

24 skeins Blue Sky Alpaca Bulky in Polar Bear, 45 yd (41m), 3½ oz (100g), 50% alpaca, 50% wool

sizes & measurements

40" (101.5cm) wide, 50" (127cm) long

» Measurements will vary slightly based on arm size, tension, and yarn choice.

yarn preparation

Combine and hold together 3 strands to create the yarn for this project. (See Arm-Knitting Yarn Preparation, page 182.)

note

» To show as much detail as possible, step-by-step photos do not include the full blanket but only a sample swatch.

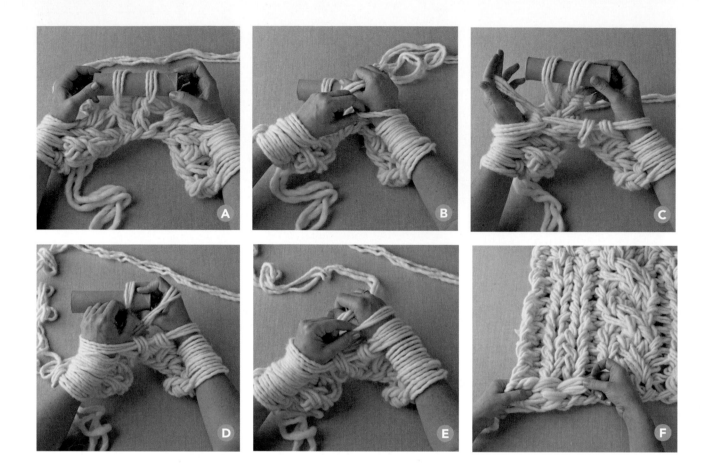

1. Cast on 32 stitches to your right arm. You need enough yarn to cast on and also to create a slip stitch border at the end, so start with a 7 yd (6.4m) tail. (After casting on all the stitches, you should have approximately a 3½ yd [3.2m] tail remaining.)

Tip: Although 32 stitches is a lot to squeeze on to your arm, it's doable. If you feel like it's too many, you may want to start with 24 stitches. The directions below would still work in the same way. However, with 24 stitches, your blanket would have 3 cables and measure approximately 30" (76cm) wide. If you change to that width, I suggest doing only 6 repeats of the 4-row pattern to keep the proportions similar to what is shown.

2. Purl 2 stitches (page 172). *Knit 4 stitches normally. Purl 1 stitch, knit 2 stitches, and purl 1 stitch. Repeat from * twice more, or until 6 stitches remain. Finally, knit 4 stitches and purl 2.

3. Purl 2 stitches. *Knit 4 stitches, purl 1 stitch, knit 2 stitches, and purl 1 stitch. Repeat from * twice more, or until 6 stitches remain. Finally, knit 4 stitches and purl 2 stitches.

4. Purl 2 stitches. *"Cable 2 back" by taking the next 2 stitches and placing them on a holder, such as a paper tube or a piece of contrasting yarn (**A**), and letting them fall to the back of the work. Knit the next 2 stitches (**B**). Then pick up the holder from the back of the work, keeping the working yarn to the left side (C), and put the 2 stitches back on your right arm (D), making sure they are oriented with the left leg of the stitch toward you and the right leg away from you. Knit those 2 stitches as usual from your right arm onto your left (E). Purl 1 stitch, knit 2 stitches, and purl 1 stitch. Repeat from * twice or until 6 stitches remain. Finally, "cable 2 back," and then purl 2 stitches.

5. Purl 2 stitches. *Knit 4 stitches, purl 1 stitch, knit 2 stitches, purl 1 stitch. Repeat from * until 6 stitches remain. Finally, knit 4 stitches, purl 2 stitches.

6. Repeat steps 2–5 seven more times, or until you reach your desired blanket length. (In knitting parlance, work the 4-row repeat 8 times total.)

. . . .

Tip: As you establish the pattern, you may find that you do not need to keep looking at the directions. Just don't forget to count the rows so you make a cable in row 3 of the 4-row pattern. Remember that you make the cables on the row when the yarn is moving from your right arm to your left on every other row going that direction.

. . . .

7. Bind off, keeping to the same pattern as the prior row, purling or knitting as you go.

8. Weave in the end from the bind off.

9. Return to the cast-on edge. Stretch the cast-on edge to match the width of the blanket.

10. Finally, take the tail from your cast-on edge and make a slip stitch border (page 179) along the bottom of the blanket to mimic the bound-off edge. Do this by pulling a loop of the tail yarn up through the space to the right of the first stitch. Work in between each knit or purled stitch from left to right, pulling the tail yarn through the blanket edge and the last loop that was made (F). When you get to the last stitch, pull the tail yarn through the last loop to finish. Weave in the end.

CHAPTER 3

PLAY

Handmade isn't just the process of turning materials into things. When children make something beautiful for themselves—something they can wrap themselves up in, play make-believe with, dig their toes into—there's a magic in that. Everyday objects become far more meaningful. Especially during playtime.

OCTOPUS FAMILY

Is it possible *not* to smile at an octopus in a bow tie? I think not. A young child will be giddy with pride to make a fuzzy friend like this for him- or herself. Or, create this wooly guy to match your friend's nursery and gift it with a color-coordinated stack of children's books.

materials

38 yd (34.5m) of "slim" or "mid" super-bulky yarn per octopus, (⑥)

Scissors

Stuffing or cotton balls

Buttons (approximately 10 mm)

Sewing needle and thread

Contrasting yarn and darning needle, for French-knot eyes (if preferred)

Ribbon or fabric for bow tie

» See pages 140–145 for an explanation of super-bulky yarns.

yarn used

1 skein Madelinetosh ASAP in Courbet's Green, Betty Draper Blue, or Cricket, 90 yd (82m), 4½ oz (127g), 100% superwash merino wool

sizes & measurements

BIG: 3" (7.5cm) wide, 10" (25.5cm) long or 3¼" (8.5cm) tall in sitting position

BABY: 2½" (6.5cm) wide, 7½" (19cm) long or 2¾" (7cm) tall in sitting position

» The big octopi's bow ties are fabric cut to 14½" x 1½" (37cm x 3.8cm) and hemmed ¼" (6mm) all the way around. The baby's tie is simply a raw-edged piece of fabric cut to 10" x ½" (25.5cm x 13mm). Ribbon or a piece of felt, or even a scrap of contrasting yarn, would work well, too.

note

» Replace the buttons with French-Knot (see Appendix, page 186) eyes to make this sea buddy safe for infants.

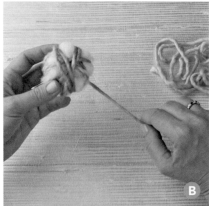

1. Finger knit a two-finger strand until it measures approximately 2½ yd (2.3m) for the adult or 2 yd (1.8m) for the baby. Bind off.

2. Cut the strand into four 21" (53.5cm) pieces for the adult or four 17" (43cm) pieces for the baby. Refinish cut strand (see Cutting a Finger-Knit Strand, page 154) (**A**). Weave all ends into the strand and trim.

. . . .

Tip: I complete steps 1 and 2 for efficiency. If it is easier for you to simply finger knit 4 pieces separately, that works, too.

. . . .

3. Take a small fistful of stuffing or cotton balls. Wrap the yarn around the stuffing as if you were winding a ball of yarn, maintaining a round shape as you go (**B**). Continue wrapping until you can't see the stuffing anymore. The wound ball should be approximately 2½" (6.5cm) for the adult or 2" (5cm) for the baby.

4. Carefully fold the 4 finger-knitted strands around the head to make the tentacles, gathering them at what will be the neck of the octopus. They should be spaced evenly, as if you were cutting a pie (**C**).

5. With a 10" (25.5cm) piece of yarn, tie the tentacles tightly underneath the head (**D**). Secure the tentacles with another knot. Trim and weave in ends.

6. Pull the tentacles down through the neck so they are snug around the octopus head. Adjust the legs around the head to your liking: spread out the overlap at the top of the head so it's not lumpy, adjust the strands so they are spaced evenly across the head, and choose a side with some character.

7. Sew the button eyes on either side of the head with a needle and thread (**E**). To make it safe for children under three, use a contrasting yarn and a darning needle to embroider French knots instead (see Appendix, page 186).

8. Tie on a bow at the neck.

9. Cuddle!

USE-EVERYWHERE BOWS

A sweet (not to mention easy) way to add a playful touch to favorite things—a tote bag, a gift, a plain coat, or even her hair—these bows are an effortless, charming upgrade requiring only a small amount of yarn. They can be attached to hair clips, buttons, headbands, or anything else that needs adornment.

PROJECT TYPE
finger knitting

SKILL LEVEL
beginner

· · · · · · · · · · · · · · ·

TECHNIQUES

materials
10 yd (9.1m) of fingering-weight yarn per bow, (**1**), combining 2 x 5-yard (4.6m) lengths

Thread to match the yarn (optional)

Barrette (optional)

tools
Darning needle

Hand-sewing needle (optional)

yarn used
1 skein Anzula Sebastian in Peach, 395 yd (361m), 4 oz (115g), 70% superwash merino, 30% SeaCell

measurements
$1\frac{1}{8}$" (2.9cm) tall, 3" (7.5cm) wide

yarn preparation
Measure and cut two 5-yd (4.6m) lengths of yarn. Combine and hold together 2 strands to create the yarn for this project.

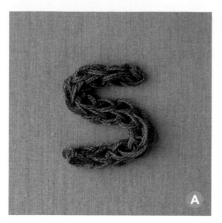

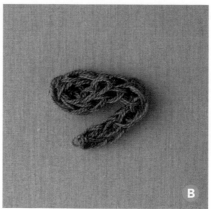

1. Finger knit a four-finger knit strand for 12 rows. Bind off and weave in ends.

2. Place the strand in a wide S shape (A).

3. Fold the top end underneath the right-hand loop (B), and fold the bottom end under the left-hand loop to form a bow.

4. Cut a 12" (30.5cm) length of yarn to wrap the center. Holding one end of this piece behind the bow, wrap the yarn around the center of the bow approximately 10 times, catching the end underneath some loops in the back as you wrap (C).

5. With a darning needle, thread the yarn underneath 3 or 4 of the wraps on the back side and pull tight. Trim the end.

6. Repeat steps 1–5 for each bow.

7. With a needle and thread, attach the bow to barette, if desired. Add more bows to your favorite coat buttons or any other accessory!

Tip: The best thing about these bows is that you can play around until you get just what you want. Try different yarn weights, holding multiple strands together, or knitting more rows before folding the bows.

At right: Pictured in the left column are bows made by finger knitting 10 rows, while the bows in the right column are made with 12 rows. The yarn weights from top to bottom are: double-stranded DK, double-stranded fingering, single-stranded worsted, single-stranded DK, double-stranded fingering, and double-stranded fingering yarns.

WIRED WORD

Add instant cool to any room with this chic graphic element. Any word. Any color. Any script. Did I mention the possibilities are endless? The texture and size of the knitting makes words pop with fun and whimsy.

PROJECT TYPE
finger knitting

SKILL LEVEL
beginner

. . . .

TECHNIQUES

materials

120 yd (109.5m) of worsted-weight yarn, (4)

7 yd (6.4m) of 24-gauge florist wire in a color to match the yarn as closely as possible

Masking tape

½" (13mm) flat-head brass nails, tacks, or removable foam adhesive strips

tools

Wire cutter

Level

Hammer

yarn used

1 skein Anzula For Better Or Worsted in Daffodil, 200 yd (183m), 4 oz (115g), 80% superwash merino, 10% cashmere, 10% nylon

» A full skein would likely allow about 4 more letters of this size.

sizes & measurements

48" (122cm) long, 13½" (34.5cm) tall (including the *b*)

1. Finger knit a four-finger strand until it measures approximately 6 yd (5.5m) or until it's long enough for your desired word.

· ·

Tip: Specified length is enough for a 13½" (34.5cm) tall *bisous*, which includes the height of the *b*. The shorter letters are approximately 6" (15cm) tall. If you want to change the dimensions of the word, simply knit less or more. Test the length by spelling out your word as you go.

· ·

2. Bind off strand. When in doubt, finger knit a longer strand that you can trim later (see Cutting a Finger-Knit Strand, page 154).

3. Make a threading loop in the wire by folding 1" (2.5cm) of the wire end over and twisting the top (**A**). This rounded shape will move more easily through the loops of the finger knitting.

4. Uncurl the tube of the finger-knitted strand, exposing the purl side of the finger knitting. Thread the wire underneath a purl stitch in the center of your strand in each row (**B**). Continue to thread the wire consistently through the same loop of each row for the entire length of finger knitting. (Be sure to thread through each row; the more rows you miss, the less consistent your line for lettering will be later.) It's okay if the strand gets slightly bunched up or twisted on the wire; it will stretch it out later.

5. When you've threaded the entire finger-knit strand, leave the wire uncut so the strand can move up and down along it as you form the word. If the wire is not on a spool, fold it such that it won't slip out of the finger knitting as you move the strand around.

6. Print out your word in large scale at a local print shop and trace the wire against the word exactly as you go (**C**). My word was 13½" x 48" (34.5cm x 122cm), using the font Quickpen by Trial by Cupcakes. (You can draw the script freehand if you prefer.)

7. Start following the text letters with the wired strand (**C**). Tape it in the critical turning points and crossover points as you go (**D**). This gives you a good sense of where things should be secured later. As you turn the strand to form the letters, keep the finger knitting straight and untwist it as you go. You want the finger knitting to lie as flat and unstretched as possible.

· ·

Tip: As the wire bends, sometimes you get an elbow of wire sticking out. In this case, soften the bend and pull the strands of finger knitting out to cover the wire.

· ·

8. Create any dots in letters, as in a lowercase *i* or *j*, by winding a small amount of yarn into a ball.

9. When you get to the end of your word, if the strand of finger knitting is too long, you can cut it and rebind it off at the appropriate length. If, for some reason, the strand is too short, adjust the letter size so that the finger-knitting strand can form all the letters required. Weave in all ends.

10. Cut the wire 1" (2.5cm) or so past the end of the word. Feed the tip of the wire through the end of the strand, turn it back and twist it around itself (**E**), and bury the wire into the strand of finger knitting.

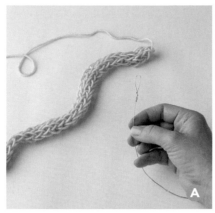

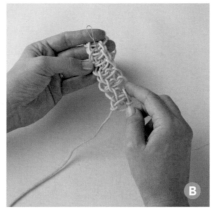

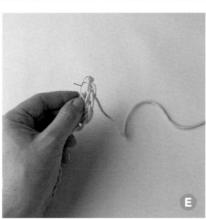

11. To hang the word, gently undo the tape from the paper. At the crossover points, use the tape to wrap around and secure the junctions for now. Set aside the finger-knit word, maintaining its form.

12. Tape the printed word to the wall where you want to hang it, level it, and hammer small flat-head brass nails into the wall in all the places needed to support the word. The nails should stick out enough to catch the wire and strand. Places to secure it include all the tops of letters and loops. Carefully remove the paper, leaving the nails intact. You may have to tear the paper.

13. Ask for help to carefully hang the word, securing the wire behind the nail heads in all the critical spots. Remove the temporary tape from the crossover points and replace with small pieces of wire or additional nails or tacks as needed. Secure the beginning and end of the word with nails or tacks as well.

Tip: If the thought of all these nail holes makes you squeamish, try using small pieces of 3M double-sided removable foam tape or Command strips. Instead of nails, use a pencil to poke through the paper and mark the critical support spots on the wall. Place small pieces of the tape on the corresponding locations on the knitted strand. Remove the backing and secure to the wall. This method may not last as long, but you'll end up with fewer wall holes.

JUMP ROPE

How to fill playtime with Old World charm? Start with vintage handles from a local garage sale or Etsy. Then simply add finger-knit cotton cording for a beautiful heirloom toy that any child will love!

PROJECT TYPE
finger knitting

SKILL LEVEL
beginner

. . . .

TECHNIQUES
Casting on....................151
Two-finger knitting 151
Binding off 151

materials

22 yd (20m) of 3mm cotton craft cording for a jump rope up to 105" (267cm)

4 large beads with 10mm holes

Jump rope handles

sizes & measurements

½" (13mm) diameter, up to 120" (305cm) long, including handles

» Test the width of your finger-knit cord to make sure it *cannot* fit through the hole in your handles and *can* fit through the hole in your beads.

notes

» You can find wooden jump-rope handles and large-holed beads in online marketplaces like Etsy. Or look for a special pair at a garage sale or antiques store.

» The correct length for a jump rope depends on the height of the jumper. Use the chart below from Jumprope.com as a guide. Measure for a good fit by standing on the middle of the jump rope and bringing both handles up. The tips of the handles should land between the armpits and shoulders. Measurements go from handle tip to handle tip.

Height of Jumper	Length of Rope
Less than 4'	72" (1.8m)
4' to 4'9"	84" (2.1m)
4'10" to 5'3"	96" (2.4m)
5'4" to 5'10"	108" (2.7m)
5'11" to 6'5"	120" (3m)

1. Leaving a 10" (25.5cm) tail, finger knit a two-finger strand until the desired length (see chart). If in doubt, plan for a longer length; you can always shorten and redo the handles to fit after, but you can't make it longer! Bind off, leaving a 10" (25.5cm) tail.

2. Thread 2 beads onto the tail about 10" (25.5cm) up the strand (**A**).

3. Next, thread the same tail through the handle. Pull the handle up to the beginning of the finger-knit strand. Tie a knot in the tail as close to the knitting as possible (**B**).

4. Slide the handle down so that the knot rests inside the top of the handle (**C**).

5. Tie a knot to use up the extra length of cord between the finger knitting and the handle. Keep the beads far enough up on the strand to be out of the way, and use the finger-knit strand as part of the initial wrapping of the knot (**D**). Push the knot into the single-strand section adjacent to the top of the handle (**E**). If you need to use up more length, tie another knot.

6. Pull the beads down to cover the knot(s). The beads should move enough to allow the jump rope to rotate easily.

7. Repeat steps 2–6 on the other end of the rope (**F**). If need be, remove the knots and handles and shorten the jump rope by undoing the bind off and unraveling the required length of stitches. Then, bind off again. When length is set, trim any tail so that it doesn't stick out of the handle.

READING NOOK

Light filled and romantic, this canopy appeals to the fairy-tale princess in all of us. Giggle and cuddle with your little ones as a blissful afternoon floats by. Or make this gauzy, glittery haven with your tween to inspire her dreams.

materials

2" (5cm) wooden cabone ring

23" (58.5cm) quilting hoop (a Hula-Hoop would work also)

2,000 yd (1,829m) of yarn in varying textures and weights for finger-knit strands and pom-poms

35 plastic novelty beads, ½" (13mm) in diameter

150 yd (137m) total of various colors of tulle from a spool, 6" (15cm) wide

40 yd (36.5m) of white ribbon, ⅜" (1cm) wide

Cardboard, for making pom-poms

Twine or embroidery thread, for tying pom-poms

tools

Ruler or tape measure

Sharp scissors

Darning needle

yarn used

1 (partial) skein Purl Soho Line Weight in Oyster Gray, 494 yd (452m), 3½ oz (100g), 100% merino wool (for 8 finger-knit strands)

1 (partial) skein Purl Soho Line Weight in Heirloom White, 494 yd (452m), 3½ oz (100g), 100% merino wool (for pom-poms)

1 skein Alchemy Silken Straw in Magnolia, 236 yd (216m), 1.4 oz (40g), 100% silk (for 5 finger-knit strands, plus the ties to the hoop)

4 skeins Blue Sky Alpaca Silk in White, 146 yd (133.5m), 1¾ oz (50g), 50% alpaca, 50% silk (for 10 finger-knit strands)

2 skeins Blue Sky Alpaca Silk in Plume, 146 yd (133.5m), 1¾ oz (50g), 50% alpaca, 50% silk (for 5 finger-knit strands)

1 skein of Purl Soho Super Soft Merino in Oyster Gray, 87 yd (79.5m), 3½ oz (100g), 100% merino wool (12 yd [11m] to string beads, and for large pom-poms)

1 (partial) skein of Manos Maxima in Oxygen, 219 yd (200m), 3½ oz (100g), 100% merino wool (for twenty 1½" [3.8cm] pom-poms)

1 skein Koigu KPM in Solid Green Blues, 175 yd (160m), 1¾ oz (50g), 100% merino wool (for 3 finger-knit strands)

sizes & measurements

24" (61cm) in diameter, 2⅔ yd (2.4m) high

note

» This is a great project to build over time. The specific yarn or materials used is not important; simply stick with a color theme. Start with a tulle base and a handful of finger-knit strands. Embellish with pom-poms, strung beads, ribbon, and additional finger-knit strands when the time or price is right.

---

1. Measure 4 strands of strong yarn, such as silk, bamboo, or twine, at 48" (122 cm) each, or the desired hanging height.

2. Tie each strand in a loop around the 2" (5cm) cabone ring (for the center) and then around the quilting hoop at even lengths (**A**). Take care not to let the strands cross each other.

3. I find it easiest to decorate the hoop after it's already hanging because you can see the effect as you go, or you can build it over time. Hang the 2" (5cm) ring with the dangling quilting hoop from a ceiling hook in your desired location, such as the corner of a room or at the head of a twin-size bed.

. . . .

Tip: Make sure the ceiling hook is well secured. Given the possibility of a child sitting on some of these strands, use a heavy-duty ceiling hook that can support more than just the weight of the canopy.

. . . .

4. Create and hang two different kinds of assorted strands (**B**) from the hoop: folded and single. The counts of strands used in the finished sample are in parentheses.

Folded strands
Create multiple 4–4⅔ yd (3.7m–4.3m) strands as materials allow. Feel free to use the following guidelines, or make up your own:

» Four-finger or two-finger knit strands in varying yarn thicknesses; weave in all ends (28 total strands).

» Strands of tulle (32 total strands)

» Strands of ribbon (8 total strands)

To attach each strand, fold it in half, place the folded part of the strand over the hoop, and pull the two ends through that folded loop (**C**).

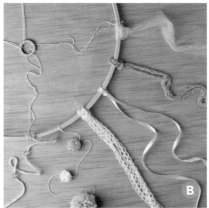

Single strands

Create 2–2⅓ yd (1.8m–2.1m) versions of the following strands:

» With a darning needle, string large beads (or bells) onto bulky yarn. Space them out at varying distances from one another (5 total strands with 7 beads each).

» Make a strand of dangling pom-poms by stringing them onto strong yarn or twine with a darning needle; see Pom-Pom Hat (page 30) for single easy pom-poms. Adjust size by changing cardboard size that you wrap around (7 total strands with pom-poms).

Tie the single strands to the hoop with a knot, trim the end, and tuck in the inside.

TASSEL DOLL BLANKET

Imagine a doll blanket so soft your child will want to sleep with it, and so plush and luxurious you'll want a grown-up version for yourself. Lucky for doll, child, and adult alike, this pattern is easily expanded to a lap throw. The blanket is made in one continuous piece—no additional stitching necessary.

materials

175 yd (160m) of worsted-weight yarn (color A), (4)

30 yd (27.5m) of worsted-weight yarn (color B), (4)

2 yd (1.8m) of scrap yarn

yarn used

1 skein Anzula For Better or Worsted in Peach, 200 yd (183m), 4 oz (115g), 80% superwash merino, 10% cashmere, 10% nylon (color A)

1 skein Anzula For Better or Worsted in Paprika, 200 yd (183m), 4 oz (115g), 80% superwash merino, 10% cashmere, 10% nylon (color B)

sizes & measurements

14½" (37cm) wide without tassels, 20" (51cm) long

technique overview

» To make the finger-knit fabric for this blanket, the finger-knit strands twist back and forth in a zigzag line connecting the new row of the finger-knitting to the prior row of the finger-knit fabric by picking up the outside row of stitches that you just made. When you turn the strand to the right, your pinky finger picks up the old stitches to join the strand (a "pinky join"). When you turn the strand to the left, your forefinger picks up the old stitches (a "forefinger join"). At the end of each width, you make some detached rows of finger knitting to help make the turn to the new row.

1. Cut and tie eighteen 4" (10.2cm) guide strands of scrap yarn loosely around color A yarn (A). These guide ties will help keep your stitch count consistent as you go.

2. Finger knit a four-finger strand in color A for 37 rows, bringing up one of the guide ties as you wrap around your forefinger for the last row (B). Finish knitting this 37th row.

. . . .

Tip: When you count rows of finger knitting (page 152), include the row on your fingers as your last row. In this pattern, you attach 34 rows of finger knitting for each width of the blanket, but you make 37 rows of finger knitting for every row of the blanket in order to complete the turn. It is this turn that makes the scallop shape.

. . . .

3. Next, with the purl side up, turn the strand to the right and toward your pinky, and put the outermost loop of the 3rd stitch away from your hand (C) onto your pinky (a pinky join). You will have 2 loops on your pinky and 1 on each of your other fingers (D).

4. Bring the yarn around your fingers to do a regular row, pulling all the bottom strands over the top as you normally would, including the lower 2 on your pinky.

5. Continue picking up 1 stitch from the next row of your already finger-knit strand with your pinky and finger knitting until you get back to the beginning of the finger-knit strand. You will have 34 attached stitches.

6. Next, finger knit 3 regular rows (detached), adding a guide tie to the last row as you wrap the yarn around your pinky (E). This is the 37th row from the last tie. To double-check, count

from the stitch after the last guide tie up to and including the stitches on your fingers.

7. Next, turn the finger-knit fabric to the left, purl side up, and pick up the 3rd stitch away from your hand with your forefinger (a forefinger join) (F); there will be 2 strands on your forefinger. Wrap the yarn for a typical row, pulling the bottom strands over the top strands, including the lower two on your forefinger.

8. Continue picking up the stitch from the next row and completing a forefinger join (G) for 34 rows, or until you get to the stitch before the tie from the prior turn. The last attached stitch will be the stitch before the tie.

9. Next, finger knit 3 rows on their own, placing a guide tie on your forefinger on the last row. Double-check your stitch count (37 stitches total from the last guide tie, including the row on your hand).

10. Turn the strand purl side up toward your pinky. Complete a pinky join row, repeating steps 3–6 (H).

11. Continue attaching your new finger-knit strand to the old until you attach the last stitch before the tie. Next, complete a forefinger join (steps 7–9).

12. Continue alternating between a pinky join and a forefinger join until you reach the desired length for the blanket. In the blanket shown, the strand was turned 18 times in total.

13. On your last join, continue to pick up stitches until the end, but do not complete the 3 detached rows. Bind off after the 34th stitch. Weave in the end. Untie and remove guide strands.

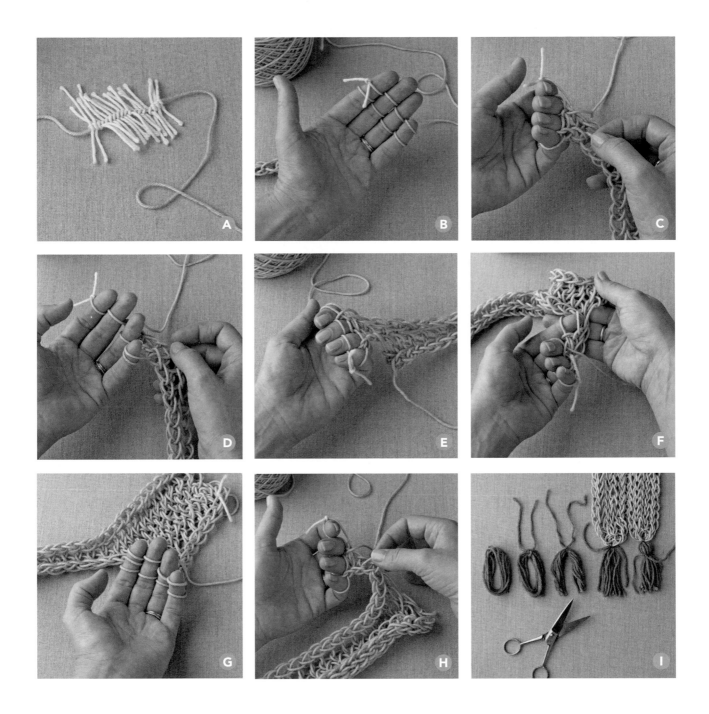

14. To make tassels (I), wrap color B around your hand 8 times. Remove the loops and tie a knot with a 7" (18cm) piece of yarn around the top of the loops. Cut the loops. Flip the tassel such that the knot is under the bend in the yarn and tie the yarn bundle to the center of the scallop. Bring one end of the tie through to the other side of the blanket. Use another 7" (18cm) piece of yarn to wrap and tie the top of the tassel ½" (13mm) down from the blanket. Knot on the back side of the tassel and trim all ties to tassel length.

WOVEN RUG

This project offers the perfect bedside rug hug for little feet. Can't you just feel the lofty finger-knit fibers squishing under your child's toes as they rub their sleepy eyes? How magical to think of that lovely texture made by your hands—or, better yet, theirs.

materials

32" x 40" (81cm x 101.5cm) Nielsen Bainbridge papermat mat board

75 yd (68.5m) of 12-ply cotton twine or 12-strand hemp yarn or other very strong fiber for warp threads

2 pieces of scrap paperboard, approximately 18" x 3" (45.5cm x 7.5 cm) each, for the shuttle

1,640 yd (1,499.5m) of multiple colors of worsted-weight yarn (4)

4½" (11.5cm) square of paperboard, for making tassels

tools

Ruler, scissors, hole punch

yarn used

5 skeins each Purl Soho Worsted Twist in Heirloom White (color A) and Extra Green (color B), 164 yd (150m), 3½ oz (100g), 100% wool

sizes & measurements

Finished rug is 26" (66cm) wide, 38" (96.5cm) long

» Expect some shrinkage from the width of the loom to the final rug width due to tension.

note

» The mat board I used has the strength for a rug of this size. Find it at your local art store for $7 a piece. Smaller rugs don't need such a loom—foam core board or cardboard would be sufficient. You can add duct tape below your loom cuts to provide reinforcement.

» The yarn or twine that is stretched the length of the loom is the *warp*. The finger-knit strand that is woven over and under the warp is called the *weft*. The *shuttle* is a tool to carry the weft across the loom's warp.

yarn preparation

This project's yarn skeins each created 10¾ yd (9.8m) of finger knitting. Weave using the entire length at one time or cut a long finger-knit strand in halves to make it more manageable.

1. Finger-knit approximately 53½ yards (49m) of four-finger strands in color A and color B each. Bind off all strands.

2. Prepare your loom by placing an even number of marks every 1" (2.5cm) along the short edge of the board (leaving extra width at the end, if necessary). Draw a line ¾" (2cm) in and parallel to the short edge. With scissors, cut to that depth at every 1" (2.5cm) mark. Repeat on the end of the board.

3. Using twine, make the warp of the loom by wrapping the twine around the board. Starting at the front and far left top, bring the twine through the notch, leaving an 8" (20.5cm) tail on the front. Bring the twine to the bottom of the board, and go in the farthest notch to the left. Bring the twine up to the top and through the farthest left slit again. You've come full circle. Now, bring the twine across the back of the loom to the next available notch in the bottom. Continue to go around the board, moving left to right, placing the twine in the next available notch at each end. Make sure the warp threads are taut across both sides of the loom without bending the board. When you fill the last notch at the top, bring the twine around and through the bottom right notch again; trim and leave an 8" (20.5cm) tail.

4. Cut two 18" x 3" (45.5cm x 7.5 cm) pieces of paperboard for shuttles. Punch a hole in the center of the end of each one. Tie a color A strand to one shuttle and a color B strand to the other.

5. This rug pattern uses 2 colors at the same time. When color A crosses the loom, color

B crosses the same direction just after it. Wherever color A goes over a warp strand, color B will go under that same warp strand. When you start, leave a 1" (2.5cm) tail of each color. Join them (page 154) by knotting them closely together (**A**).

6. As you turn to weave in the opposite direction, bring color A under color B to start the next row. At the next turn, bring color B under color A at the edge. Continue to alternate this way as you weave (**B**).

. . . .

Tip: As you pull the strands through the loom, the strands will have quite a bit of tension. When there is no more slack in the strand, bring a just-enough length of the working strand back across the loom the way you came so that the strands don't feel stretched out. In this way, you remove the tension from the strand as it sits under and over the warp. If the sides of the rug start to move in toward the center, the tension of the strands in the loom is too tight.

. . . .

7. Continue weaving, joining finger-knit strands (page 154) as your length runs out. Joins can fall anywhere across the loom. Keep the finger knitting dense enough to cover the warp threads and the loom so the board doesn't show through, approximately 30 strands across 10" (25.5cm) of length.

8. At the end, cut each strand 2" (5cm) longer than the loom and rebind off (page 154). Join the strands (**C**). Adjust weaving tension to fit any excess length. Weave in any ends.

9. Flip your loom over and cut the warp ties (**D**), trimming length to 6" (15cm).

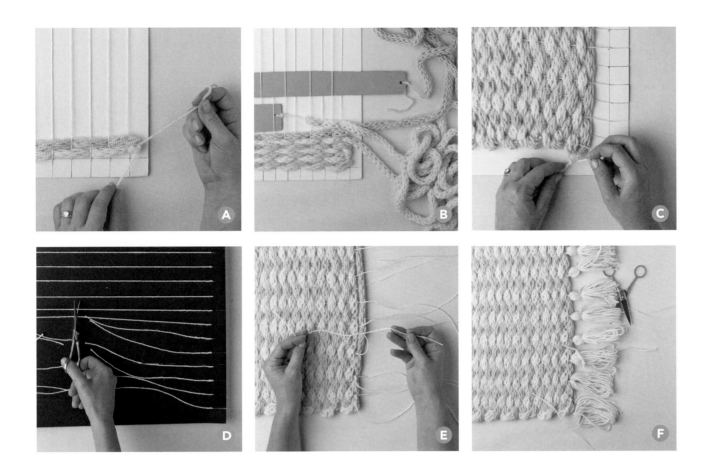

10. Remove the loom. Tie all the warp ties together in pairs (**E**).

11. Make tassels at each warp tie (**F**). Wrap yarn around a 4½" (11.5cm) square of paperboard 15 times. Remove the loops and tie them to a set of warp cords. Use a 6" (15cm) piece of yarn to tie a knot around the loops (including the warp cords) approximately ½" (13mm) away from the rug. Wrap the tie around the loops a couple times and knot. Cut the bottom of the loops, and trim all strands. Repeat for each pair of warp ties.

❯❯ Change the size of the loom and determine how much finger knitting you need with this formula:

Finished length x finished width = A

A ÷ 1,280 = B

B x 107 = approximate yards of finger knitting required

❯❯ Construct a loom to fit a specific length of finger knitting by following this formula:

Length of finger-knit strand ÷ 107 = C

$\sqrt{C}$ x 32" (81cm) = suggested width of loom

$\sqrt{C}$ x 40" (101.5cm) = suggested length of loom

❯❯ This assumes you are using a worsted-weight yarn and that the density and tension of your weaving are similar to mine.

PRINCESS CROWN

This delicate gold-wire crown sparkles with magic and dreams. Flowing tulle and dangling jewels transform a simple knit band into the perfect accessory for a world of make-believe for children of any age. I might just wear one myself this coming Halloween.

PROJECT TYPE
finger knitting

SKILL LEVEL
intermediate

• • • • • • • • • • • • •

TECHNIQUES

Casting on 151

Two-finger knitting 151

Binding off 151

Weaving in ends 154

materials

6 yd (15m) of 22-gauge gold wire

18" (46cm) of 26-gauge wire to make the dangling beads

8mm crystal beads

12 yd (11m) of tulle from a spool, 6" (15cm) wide

note

» Feel free to play with the materials to make this crown. Try beads ranging from 6mm to 12mm. Or try a higher gauge wire. The crown will be more pliable but won't keep its shape as well.

tools

Wire cutter

Needle-nose pliers

sizes & measurements

2" (5cm) tall, size to fit wearer 19" to 23" (48cm to 58cm) circumference

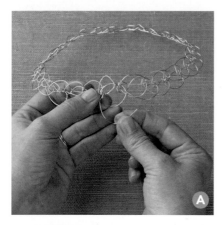

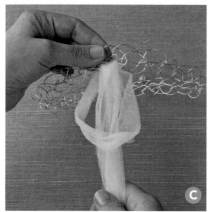

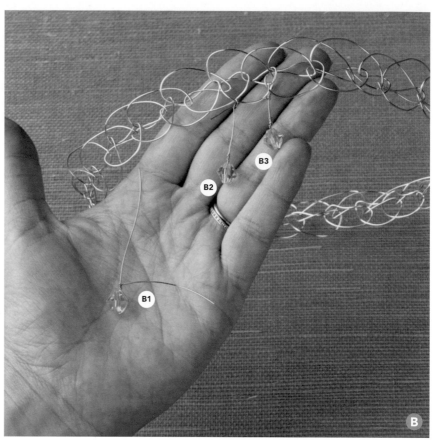

Tip: With stiff material like wire, it will help to work either mid finger or close to your fingertips as opposed to working at the bottom of your fingers. It is stiff stuff, so you will want to keep it fairly loose and leave yourself some room to maneuver as you wrap around your fingers. It is helpful to pull the finger-knit strand flat as you go.

1. Finger knit a two-finger strand with 22-gauge wire. Pull the strand flat as you go until it measures the circumference of the wearer's head (between 19" and 23" [48.5cm and 58.5cm]).

2. Bind off the stitches on your finger and cut the wire, leaving a 4" (10cm) tail.

3. Bring the beginning of the strand and the end of the strand together (**A**). Use the tail to weave in and out of the beginning and end to complete the circle of the crown.

4. To add beads to the front, use the thinner wire. Thread a crystal bead on a 4" (10cm) piece of wire. Holding the bead mid-way on the wire, fold the wire up over the bead. Twist it 3 times around the other end of the wire (**B1**), pressing the loops close to the bead. Cut the wire and twist the remaining length with pliers. Repeat twice to make 3 wired beads in this same manner.

5. Attach the first wired bead to the middle of the crown by threading the wire holding the bead through the hole made by 2

overlapping stitches. Fold the wire so that the bead will dangle 1½" (3.8cm) (**B2**). Wrap the tail of the wire around the main shaft coming out the bead at least 3 times close to the crown. Cut the wire and finish wrapping with the needle-nose pliers.

6. On either side of the center bead, add the other 2 beads, folding the wire so that those beads dangle less than the center one. Trim and wrap the wire accordingly (**B3**).

7. To add tulle to the back (**C**), cut seven 1.5 yd (1.4m) strands of 6" (15cm) tulle. Fold a piece of tulle in half lengthwise. Thread the folded part through one of the wire circles at the base of the crown. Pull the tails of the tulle through the loop. Repeat for each strand of tulle.

PRINCE CROWN

Your prince is treated no less magnificently in a gold crown of his own, bedecked with jewels. This crown pattern includes advanced techniques, including attached finger knitting and finger knitting with beads, which allows for the fabulous crown shape and embedded jewels. Try the Princess Crown (page 127) first to practice finger knitting with wire.

PROJECT TYPE
finger knitting

SKILL LEVEL
advanced

. . . .

TECHNIQUES

Casting on.....................151

Two-finger knitting 151

Binding off 151

Weaving in ends 154

materials

Six 8mm crystal beads

Three 12mm crystal beads

13 yd (11.9m) of 24-gauge gold wire

» Feel free to play with the materials to make this crown. Try beads ranging from 6mm to 12mm. Or try a higher gauge wire; the crown will be more pliable but won't keep its shape as well.

tools

Wire cutter

sizes & measurements

Small, Medium, Large

3" (7.5cm) tall, 20.5" (21.5", 22.5")/
52cm (55cm, 57cm) circumference

1. String the crystal beads on the wire in the following order: small, large, small, small, large, small, small, large, small. This will allow the large bead to end up on the point of the crown. Let them fall toward the end of the wire (although don't let them fall off!).

2. Finger knit a two-finger strand for 31 (Small), 33 (Medium), or 35 (Large) rows. It helps to pull the finger-knit strand away from your hand as you work and make it flat.

3. When you reach the desired number of rows, bring the end of the strand into a circle toward you. The purl side will be on the outside of the circle (remember that coming off your fingers, the knit side of finger knitting faces your hand, the purl side faces out). Place the left, outside stitch of the beginning of the strand on your middle finger (A).

4. Wrap the wire around your fingers and pull the two bottom-most strands over the top strand on your middle finger. This is attached finger knitting in the round. Continue to move around the circle of the first row of finger knitting, attaching each new row of finger knitting you make to the next stitch from the previous round.

5. Knit for 12 (Small), 13 (Medium), or 14 (Large) rows of finger knitting. For the last attached row of this set of stitches, feed 1 crystal bead up onto your forefinger (B). Finger knit this row as usual (C).

6. To complete the prong, knit 3 rows on their own (not attached). For the first 2 rows of these, add a bead to your finger as described above (D). The largest bead should be in the middle of this set of 3 (E).

7. Skip 1 stitch/row on the prior round (F) and finger knit two attached rows, the last one with a small bead around your forefinger (G).

8. Repeat steps 6 and 7 (H).

9. Repeat step 8 one more time, without the bead in step 7.

10. Finger knit the remaining rows as attached rows.

11. Cut your wire with the wire cutter, leaving an 8" (20.5cm) tail. Bind off your strand. Bring both tails toward the center of the crown and weave in the ends (I).

12. Pull the largest bead and each prong up to a point. Shape the prongs. If necessary, you can twist the largest bead so it's trapped in the wire at the highest point.

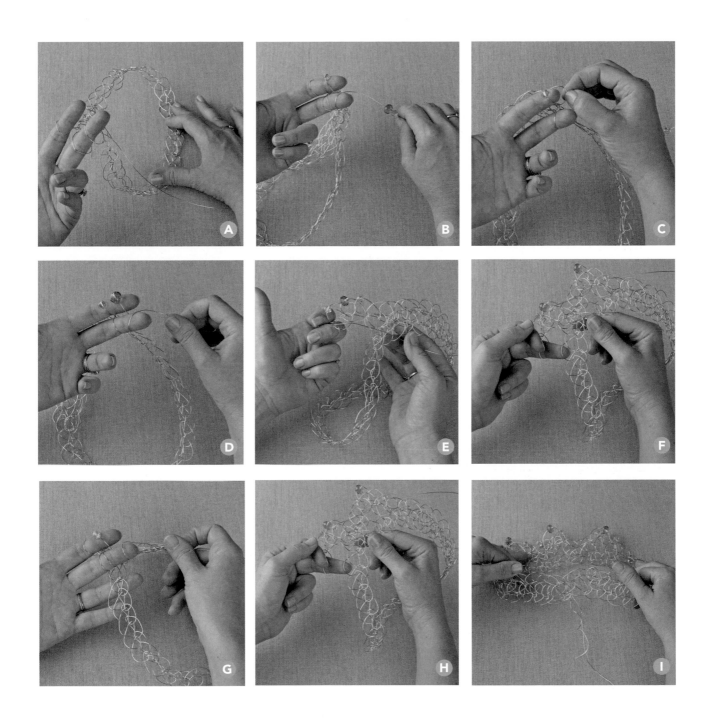

BABY BOOTIES

You're never too young for luxurious baby alpaca. These incredibly soft booties were born to keep baby's feet warm in style. With felt soles stitched to the bottom and unique embroidery-thread bling topping each pair, everything about these booties tells the receiver how much you care.

PROJECT TYPE
finger knitting

SKILL LEVEL
advanced

· · · · · · · · · · · · · · ·

TECHNIQUES

Casting on....................148

Four-finger knitting......149

Binding off 150

Weaving in ends 154

materials

22 yd (20m) of worsted-weight yarn per pair, (4)

Sole template (page 187)

100% wool felt in complementary color

½" (13cm) elastic (optional)

1 skein of embroidery floss (optional)

tools

Pen, pencil, or stitch holder

Needle

Air-soluble fabric marker (optional)

materials used

1 skein each in Ballet Pink, Artemisia Green, Ice Blue, Sea Salt, and Heirloom White of Purl Soho Alpaca Pure, 109 yd (100m), 3½ oz (100g), 100% alpaca

1 skein each in Ecru, 352, and 597 of DMC size 5 pearl cotton embroidery thread 27 yd (25m), 100% cotton

1 skein DMC Mouliné Color Variations embroidery thread in color 4170 8.7 yd (8m), 100% long-staple Egyptian cotton

1 Purl Soho Wollfilz Felt Bundle in Anemone for all felt in pictured booties

sizes & measurements

2½" (6.5cm) wide, 4¼" (11cm) long

1. Finger knit a four-finger knit strand for 18 rows.

2. Remove the stitches from your fingers; if preferred, place them on a pencil or stitch holder. Carefully flip the strand over and put the stitches back on your fingers (A). The loop that was on your forefinger when it came off will now be on your pinky, and vice versa. Make sure the working yarn is coming from between your ring and pinky finger.

3. Now you will complete a forefinger join, which will turn the strand to attach new rows to the old rows. Turn your hand toward the finger-knit strand and place the outermost stitch in the second row away from your hand onto your forefinger (B).

4. Move the working yarn back to its usual location by bringing it behind your ring finger and over your middle finger (C).

5. Now, wrap the working yarn as you typically would to finger knit a row. You will have 3 strands on your first 2 fingers (D). Complete knitting that row, bringing the bottom 2 strands over the top strand where necessary.

6. On the next and every following row, pick up the outermost stitch from the next row, place it on your forefinger, and finger knit a row. Because the strand flipped midway, your strand will be half facing up and half facing down (E).

7. When you get back to the beginning, bind off and knot the 2 tails to bring the beginning and the end together (F). Pull the piece lengthwise so the stitches settle in place. Weave in ends.

8. Repeat steps 1–8 to make the second bootie top.

9. Copy and cut out the sole template (see Appendix, page 187). Trace and cut 2 soles from the wool felt.

10. Orient the bootie top with the cast-on and bound-off edges to your right and the turn to your left (G). The piece will be splayed out a little more on the wrong side. If the wrong side is facing up, flip it over (keeping bound-off end to your right) so that the small rolling side is at the top.

11. Overlap the ends of each bootie top. Make one bootie with the right side on top, and one with the left side on top (H). Place these shapes on top of the felt sole and pin them in place.

12. Holding the sole in place as you go, use embroidery thread and the blanket stitch (see Appendix, page 186) (I), to sew the upper to the sole. The blanket stitches should be about ⅛" (3mm) apart. Stitch freehand or use an air-soluble fabric marker to mark the sole with dots to guide your stitches.

13. Sew the flaps together where they overlap 1" (2.5cm) down from the opening. Bury the stitch in the yarn (I1). If desired, run elastic through the open stitches under the roll at the top of the bootie.

14. Embellish the booties with embroidery thread decorations as shown on page 134.

» Create the looped bows on the blue booties by wrapping thread around two fingers 15 times. Remove thread from fingers and wrap thread around center of the bundle multiple times. Secure with a few half hitches (see page 27, step 7).

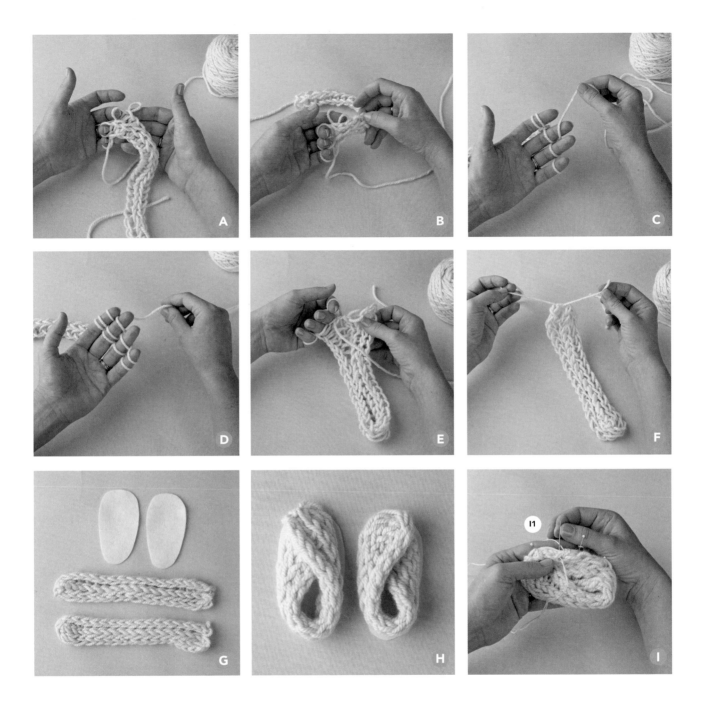

» Cut the loop ends on the bow to make the tasseled bow on the cream booties.

» See Pom-Pom Hat (page 32) for single, easy pom-poms (just miniaturize!) as shown on the green booties.

» The tassels on the pink booties are finished the same way as the tassels for the Tassel Doll Blanket (page 119).

» The detail on the taupe bootie is made by stitching around the top roll of the back for 1". Have fun!

CHAPTER 4

HOW-TO

Learning how to finger and arm knit may seem challenging at first glance, but without needles or a hook to struggle with, you may be surprised at how easy it is to pick up both techniques. The speed with which you can make things is a pleasure, too—a little instant gratification never hurt anyone.

Materials, Yarn & Gauge

For most of the patterns in this book you will need scissors and a measuring tape or ruler. Any specialized tools required for additional sewing or crafting are listed in the individual patterns.

For each project you'll find a subheading at the top—Materials—that will tell you the general weight category and amount of yarn you need to make each project.

Generally, the projects in this book can be recreated by simply using a similar size yarn (both in weight and length)—no other calculations required. For a handful of projects, when size of the finished piece is important, you may want to check the gauge of your knitting (see Troubleshooting Arm Knitting, page 184.)

Choosing Yarn by Weight

Shelves and shelves of yarn can be daunting, whether you're physically in the store or in the endless virtual Internet aisles of yarn. Which yarn should you choose for your project? Don't feel confined by the yarn I used! Try to see those jammed shelves as a good thing—look at all the fabulous yarn choices out there to make beautiful things with. Especially the ones on sale! Just find yarn that's a similar weight.

Yarn comes in different weights and is made up of various fibers (wool, cotton, silk, etc.). The *weight* refers to the thickness of the yarn and ranges from super fine to jumbo.

Yarn Weight Categories

The Craft Yarn Council has standardized yarn weights into seven categories. Sometimes yarns are packaged in a skein and labeled with one of these seven numbered symbols:

1. Super fine, baby, fingering, sock
2. Fine baby, sport
3. Light, DK, light worsted
4. Medium, afghan, Aran, worsted
5. Bulky, chunky, craft, rug
6. Super bulky, bulky, roving
7. Jumbo, roving

Experienced knitters and yarn-shop owners casually use the above common names to describe yarns. Don't be intimidated, they are just talking about how thick a yarn is.

Yarn Gauge

The other way you'll see yarn weight shown on labels is the gauge label. In traditional knitting, each category of yarn knits up within an expected range of stitches per inch when using a specific needle. In this book, that range of stitches isn't something you'll use for finger knitting or arm knitting, but it is a tool that can help you choose a yarn similar to the one I used for each project.

If picking out your own yarn instead of using what I chose, pay attention to the stated "stitches per inch" category and make sure it matches the range listed on your yarn's label. Your yarn's label may show the gauge over 4 inches, in which case you would multiply the stitches per inch by 4 and compare. This will help you achieve similar results.

Yarn Categories

This chart outlines the yarn and materials used in this book from thinnest to thickest, along with their categories, their names, and typical knitting gauges.

Craft Yarn Council Yarn Category	Yarn Name or Other Material	Traditional Knitting Stitches per Inch (over 4")	Projects in Book
	26- to 18-gauge wire		Princess Crown (page 127), Prince Crown (page 131)
	1 mm cord, twine, or rope		Hemp Twine Necklace (page 25)
1 Super Fine	Baby, fingering, sock	6.75–8 (27–32)	Use-Everywhere Bows (page 103), Reading Nook (page 114)
2 Fine	Baby, sport	5.75–6.5 (23–26)	Linen Baskets (page 89)
3 Light	DK (double knit), light worsted	5.25–6 (21–24)	Reading Nook (page 114)
4 Medium	Worsted, afghan, Aran	4–5 (16–20)	Baby Booties (page 135), Wired Word (page 107), Woven Rug (page 122), Tassel Doll Blanket (page 119), Covered Stool (page 69), Cashmere Scarf (page 48), Double-Strand Headband (page 21)
5 Bulky	Chunky, craft, rug	3–3.75 (12–15)	Color-Block Scarf (page 29), Statement Necklace (page 17)
	3mm cord, twine, or rope		Jump Rope (page 111), Two-Tone Dog Collar (page 37)
6 Super Bulky	"Slim" super bulky, roving	2.75 (11)	Pom-Pom Hat (page 32), Beanie Hat (page 45), Infinity Cowl (page 13) , Slouch Hat (page 40), Lace Pillows (page 81), Octopus Family (page 98), Giant Monogram (page 73)
	"Mid" super bulky, roving	2.25–2.5 (9–10)	Infinity Cowl (page 13)
	"Big" super bulky, roving	1.75–2 (7–8)	Oversized Pillows (page 61), Cabled Blanket (page 92), Faux Sheepskin (page 85), Purl-Side Tote (page 53), Infinity Cowl (page 13)
	¼" (6mm) rope		Rope Rug (page 65)
7 Jumbo	Jumbo, roving	1.5 and fewer (6 and fewer)	Grand Pouf (page 77)

Four Finger

Bulky-weight yarn

100% cotton macramé cord

Worsted-weight yarn

Doubled fingering-weight yarn

DK-weight yarn

Choosing Yarn for Finger Knitting

Finger knitting can use a broad range of yarn weights, but generally it works and looks best in categories (4) and higher. Thinner yarns can work if they are super fuzzy or super stiff, or if you hold multiple strands together. A yarn's fiber composition and weight can completely change the overall look of a project, so feel free to experiment. These swatches include finger-knit fibers in different weights and materials, knit in both two- and four-finger strands.

Two Finger

Doubled fingering-weight yarn

DK-weight yarn

Worsted-weight yarn

Bulky-weight yarn

⅛" (3mm) rope

Choosing Yarn for Arm Knitting

Arm-knit fabric can be made with a range of yarn weights, but most typically they are yarns that are in category (6) (super bulky) or (7) (jumbo). These categories of yarn include a broad range of yarn weights. I split category (6) into three subcategories for this book to help you choose the right weight for the project:

- "slim" super bulky
- "mid" super bulky
- "big" super bulky

To create a rich and full fabric, ply multiple strands of these yarns together and work with them at the same time.

The number of strands you ply and the type of yarn you use will influence the size of your stitches and your resulting fabric.

5 strands chunky

6 strands "slim" super bulky

8 strands "slim" super bulky

3 strands "big" super bulky

4 strands "big" super bulky

3 strands ¼" (6mm) cotton rope

2 strands jumbo

Finger Knitting 101

At its heart, finger knitting is simply using your fingers to create a series of loops strung together. Technically, if you use all four fingers, the material you are knitting has 4 stitches per row (one on each finger). You can finger knit with one finger (making a chain), or with two, or three, in which case your rows have 1 to 3 stitches per row.

When you finger knit, you are making two sides to the fabric. One side is the purl side, one side is the knit side. Here are other terms you'll come across in every finger knit project in this book.

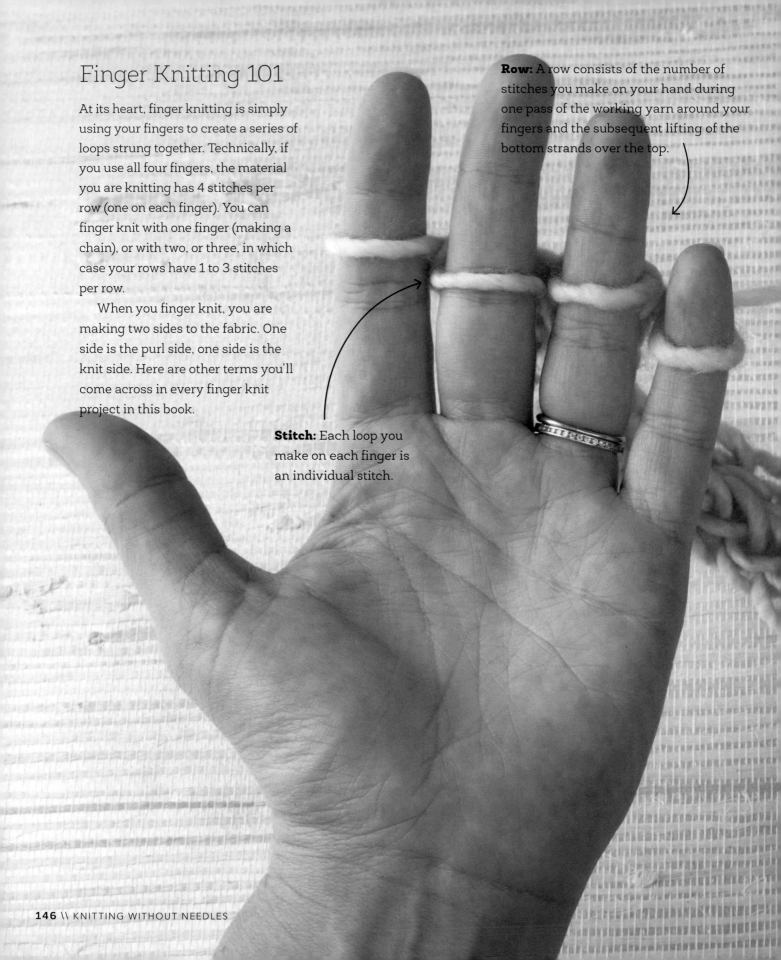

Row: A row consists of the number of stitches you make on your hand during one pass of the working yarn around your fingers and the subsequent lifting of the bottom strands over the top.

Stitch: Each loop you make on each finger is an individual stitch.

Working Yarn: Extending from the ball of yarn you are working with, the working yarn is used to make new stitches.

Tail: The yarn left over from casting on (page 148) your stitches is called the tail.

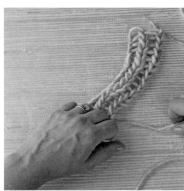

Knit Side

This is the side of the fabric that faces your hand as you knit.

Purl Side

This is the opposite side of the fabric, which faces away from your hand as you knit.

Pulling Strand Taut

Pulling on the tail straightens the strand. The tension causes the sides to curve in toward one another, forming a tube.

Four-Finger Knitting

This is the most common type of finger knitting. As the name implies, you will wrap yarn over four fingers to create stitches.

Finger knitting works in an over-under pattern. If you've gone over a finger last, you'll go under or behind the next one.

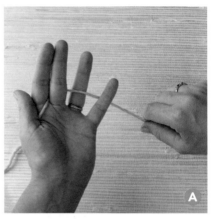

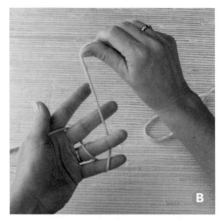

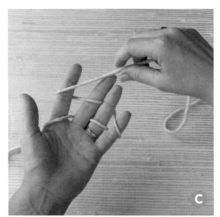

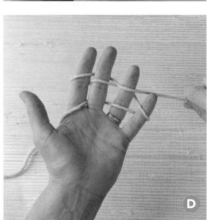

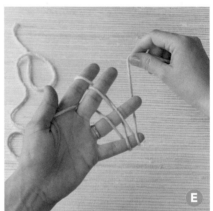

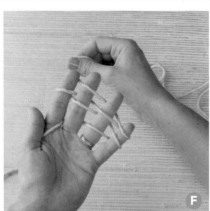

Casting On

Start by placing the yarn in between your thumb and palm-up hand, letting the tail hang behind your hand. Bring the working yarn between your forefinger and your middle finger to the back of your hand. Beginners may choose to cast on and knit with the stitches at the base of the finger; however, it is faster and will give you more consistency if you knit higher up on your fingers.

Bring the tail from behind your middle finger to the front of your hand and over your

ring finger (A). Wrap the yarn around your pinky, and head back the other direction, going behind your ring finger and over your middle finger (B). Next, bring the yarn around your forefinger (C). Bring the yarn behind your middle finger and over your ring finger (D) and around your pinky (E). Next, bring the yarn behind your ring finger, and over your middle finger (F). Each finger should have 2 wraps on it (include the tail hanging over your forefinger). You've now cast on.

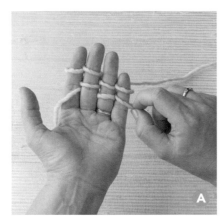

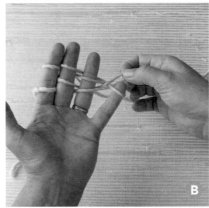

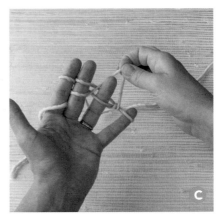

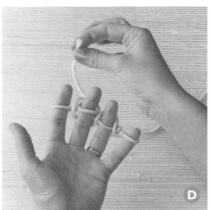

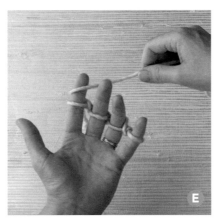

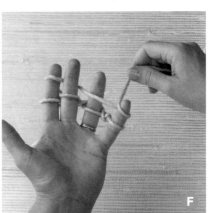

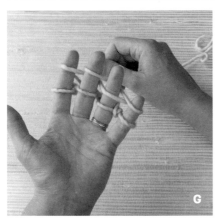

Knitting

Row 1: Starting with your pinky finger, pick up the lower strand (A), and bring it over the top strand and the top of your pinky (B). Next, pick up the lower strand on your ring finger and bring it over the top strand and the top of your finger (C). Repeat for your middle finger. Pick up the tail, which is lying across your forefinger, and bring it in between your forefinger and middle finger (D) to the back of your hand. Now that you've moved the tail to the back, for future rows, the strand on your forefinger will be tighter around your finger like the rest of the stitches. If the stitches ride up your fingers, just push them lower.

  Row 2: Rethread the working yarn across your fingers. Bring the working yarn around your forefinger and behind your middle finger (E), then over your ring finger and around your pinky (F), and finally behind your ring finger and over your middle (G). You should have two strands on each finger. Now pull the lower strands over the top as described in row 1.

Stopping in the Middle

To take a break in the middle of finger knitting, feed a pencil, pen, stitch holder, or large safety pin (**A**) through the loops from your pinky to your forefinger, moving from right to left (**B**). Set the work aside (**C**).

When you want to pick it up again, place the loops back on your fingers, starting with the forefinger and moving from the left back to the right. The knit side should be facing your hand (see page 147).

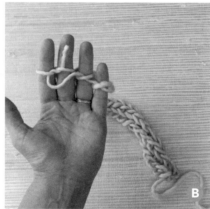

Binding Off

To bind off, cut the working yarn (**A**) and bring the end through your pinky loop, your ring finger loop, your forefinger loop, and, lastly, your middle finger loop (**B**); this is where the working yarn is extending from,

so it is the last loop you want to tighten down. Holding on to the working yarn, remove the stitches from your fingers. Pull the working yarn slowly (**C**), and the loops should close fairly evenly.

Two-Finger Knitting

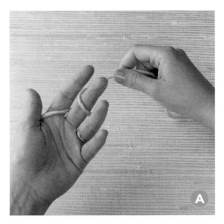

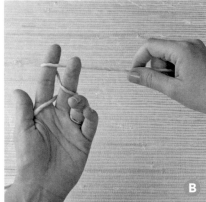

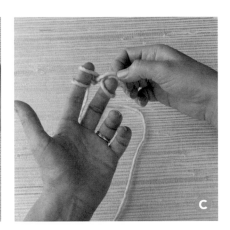

Casting On and Knitting

Two-finger knitting works the same way as knitting with four fingers, only you are wrapping over and under just two of your fingers, your forefinger and middle finger, for a narrower chain. The strand comes out looking more square in shape.

Cast on by holding the tail between your thumb and forefinger. Bring the working yarn around your middle finger (A), then behind and around your forefinger (B).

Lastly, bring the working yarn behind and around your middle finger.

Knit a row in the same way as for four-finger knitting but start with your middle finger (C). Bring the lower strand over the upper strand and over the top of the finger. Repeat on the forefinger. Restrand the top row so there are 2 strands on each finger again. Repeat from the beginning.

Binding Off

To bind off, cut the working yarn and bring the end through your forefinger loop, then the middle finger loop (A). Pull the working yarn (B) and remove the stitches from your fingers. Slowly pull the working yarn taut.

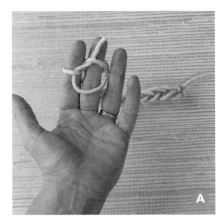

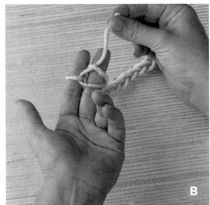

One-Finger and Three-Finger Knitting

Though these techniques are not included in the projects in this book, they can be useful in your finger-knitting repertoire.

To finger knit with one finger, cast on by placing a slip knot (page 162) around your forefinger. Wrap the yarn around your forefinger and pull the lower loop over the top. Repeat, making a one-finger chain of stitches. Bind off by cutting and bringing the working yarn through the loop on your finger. Use one-finger stitches to make simple bracelets, headbands, or embellishments.

To finger knit with three fingers, the process is similar to the previous instructions for two- and four-finger knitting in that you follow an over-and-under pattern around your fingers, leaving your pinky out of the process. Three-finger knitting is a more advanced concept, but it can be useful for decreasing stitches in a fabric, from four-finger down to two-finger knitting.

how to count rows

To count rows in finger knitting, count from the first stitch above the tail up to, and including, the row on your fingers. The finger-knit strand below has 20 rows.

a tip on tension

As you knit, the strand will naturally be tighter coming off your pinky than coming off your index finger because of your finger size and the way the yarn is wrapped around your fingers. This difference in tension will cause your strand to curve as you knit.

The "pulled taut" purl strand below has been flattened a little to show you the purl side. In its pulled natural state, that side will be hidden inside the curl of the knit side. Typically, and in almost all the patterns, the finger knitting is pulled taut as you go. The patterns in this book will specify if the strand shouldn't be pulled.

The two sides—purl and knit—are always there. Pull the sides apart to reveal the purl side of the strand. The thicker the yarn, the easier this is to see and find.

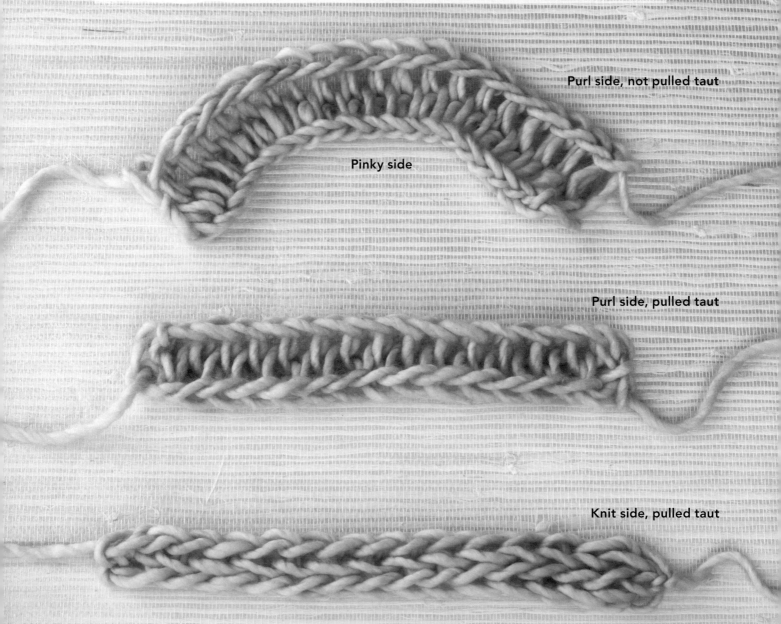

Purl side, not pulled taut

Pinky side

Purl side, pulled taut

Knit side, pulled taut

Finishing Your Finger Knitting

Weaving in Ends (top)
To weave in an end of finger knitting, simply bring the tail back through the purl side of the finger-knit strand and weave it under the loops. To make it more secure, you can then weave it back the other direction.

Cutting a Finger-Knit Strand (middle)
Occasionally you may need to cut a finger-knit strand in the middle or trim part of the strand off. Whether you're cutting finger knitting to fit a certain size, to cover something exactly, or you want multiple pieces of your strand, don't be afraid! It is easy to do.

Use scissors to cut the finger-knit strand right in the middle of it, anywhere you like. Keep in mind that you will lose about an inch (2.5cm) in length from each side after you rebind the strand. Remove the cut pieces; one end will look as if you pulled it off your fingers mid strand (**A**). Loosen the stitches or pull out a row or two until you have enough working yarn to thread it through the open stitch loops (**B**). The other end will close tight when you simply pull on the strand of yarn emerging from the loose pieces (**C**).

Joining a Finger-Knit Strand (bottom)
To join a finger-knit strand, tie the two tails of the strands together with a square knot, bringing the ends of the finger-knit strand as close to each other as possible (**A**), even overlapping them a bit. Weave the ends back into the strands (**B**).

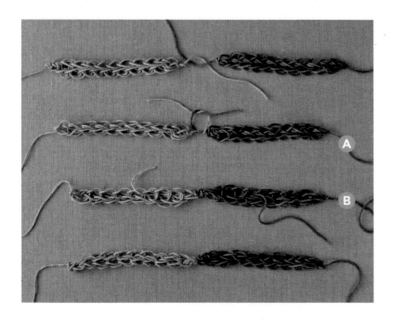

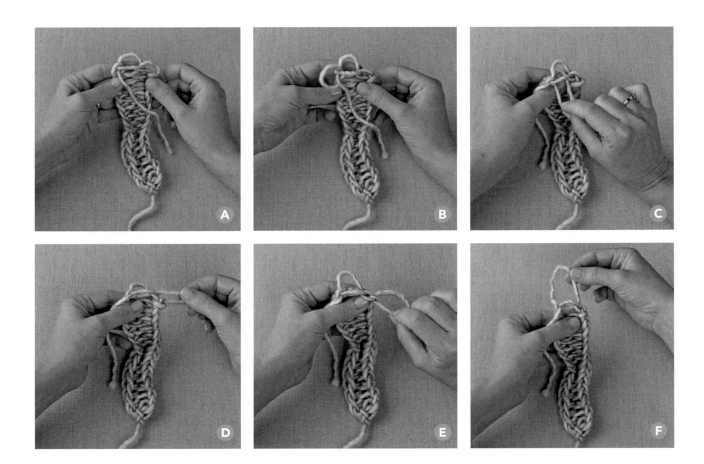

Tightening Strand Ends

When you finger knit, the beginning of your strand can start off a little looser than the main body of the strand, and sometimes the end can have extra loops or bulges. Some of the time, the tightness of your finger-knitting ends doesn't matter very much, but sometimes it will be important for the beginning of the finger-knit strand to be even with the rest of the strand or for the end to have a nice finish.

To tighten the end of your strand, simply pull slowly and evenly as you bind off your stitches and don't forget to go through the loop on your middle finger last.

Tightening the beginning of your strand looks more complicated than it is. You're basically tightening the first round of stitches you made when you started. It flows from place to place once you start, but these photos will help you keep your place.

Return to the beginning of the strand with the purl side facing up (A). Start by picking up the loop farthest to the left, which has curled around the side of the strand. Pull it toward you (B). Next, pull on the stitch in the middle of the strand to tighten the loop you just made (C). This yarn flows to the back; tighten this stitch (D). This will flow into the small loop around the edge of the right side (E). Continue to follow this strand, tightening along the top row (F) and eventually getting to the tail, which you can pull taut. Pull on the sides a little so the beginning is even with the width of the rest of the strand. Beautiful!

Knitting Wider (or Attached Finger Knitting)

Once I started designing finger-knitting projects, the question readers asked the most was this: "Is there any way to make a wider fabric?"

I gave a lot of thought and practice to this question. After trying many different ways to attach finger-knitted strands together, I developed three ways, shown below, to build a larger fabric. Frankly, I got super excited! The concept of making a full knit fabric using just your fingers propels the craft from simple embellishment into a world of beautiful, stand-alone pieces. Enjoy!

« Single-Strand Attached Finger Knitting
This is a finger-knit strand that attaches back to itself in a snake-like pattern, turning to the right, then the left, then the right for as many times as desired. Find this technique in the Tassel Doll Blanket (page 119), which includes a full tutorial.

Spiral Attached Finger Knitting »
This is a finger-knit strand that spirals out from a center. You join the finger-knit strand back to itself as you increase stitches to maintain a smooth and growing spiral circumference. This technique is used to make the Linen Baskets (page 89).

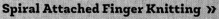

« Multistrand Attached Finger Knitting
This technique is a way to attach finger-knit strands in a straight line. Each individual stripe is its own strand that begins and ends at each side of the piece, leaving more ends to weave in. This technique is used in the Cashmere Scarf (page 48).

Reverse Finger-Knit Border

Completing the more advanced finger-knit techniques by adding a border gives your piece a nice finished look. The border evens out the ends and edges. Also, finger knitting a border that rolls in the opposite direction from the main piece's finger-knit strands helps the overall piece remain flat. You can use this technique to finger knit a border around any of the attached finger-knitting techniques (page 156). You can complete the reverse border with either a two-finger or a four-finger strand. See the Cashmere Scarf (page 48) for instructions.

Blocking Wider Pieces

If you are completing a finger-knit piece to wear, blocking the piece is a good idea. Blocking relaxes the fibers that you've finger knit and settles them in their place a bit. It helps relax the curl that finger knitting naturally takes on.

To block a piece, submerge it in cool water. Let it sit for up to an hour to absorb the water. Do not agitate the piece, especially if you knit with 100 percent wool. Gently squeeze out the excess water but do not wring or twist it. Lay the piece on a large bath towel and roll the towel up from the bottom. Let the towel absorb even more water. Then lay the piece out on a blocking board or on a clean carpeted area. Pin the piece down with rustproof T-pins to the desired size and shape. Let dry.

tips and best practices

» After the initial cast on in a finger-knit strand, pull the tail to tighten the beginning of the strand—not too much, though, or it will be too hard to knit!

» Unless specified, the working yarn should always come from the loop around your middle finger, exiting from between your middle and forefinger.

» Always lift strands starting at your pinky and moving toward your forefinger.

» Don't tug too much extra length into the bottom strands as you lift them over your fingers. Knitting at mid finger is the best way to limit this extra length and create neater looking stitches.

» Pull the working yarn slowly as you tighten the bound-off stitches to end a strand.

Troubleshooting Finger Knitting

Here are some of the most common questions and concerns I receive from my blog and teaching experience. Remember that it takes time and practice to master a new skill or craft, so be patient with yourself. You will soon get it, and your work will be beautiful!

Frequently Asked Questions

What if the beginning of the strand is too loose?
Try to keep the beginning of the strand tighter, pulling the tail a little when you cast on to tighten the beginning. Or follow Tightening Strand Ends (page 155) after the strand has been bound off.

Why is the working yarn coming from my pinky or somewhere else and/or why doesn't it pull easily or feel right?
This can happen due to a few different reasons, and here are some options to try.

» Most often, the problem is that the working yarn has slipped off your middle finger inadvertently. Try bringing the working yarn over your middle finger and lift the bottom strand over the top. Finish knitting any other double strand that might

appear on your other fingers. This should make the work ready for the beginning of the next row.

» Sometimes the problem stems from not putting the knitting back on your fingers properly after taking a break. Check that you have the strand oriented the right way, with the knit side (page 147) facing your hand.

» If things still seem off, slowly pull the working yarn out of each stitch (removing stitches from your finger if you need to). Place the revealed loops on your fingers one-by-one until the working yarn ends up emerging from the loop on your middle finger. Then, start again.

What if my forefinger or pinky edge is loose?

Hold your forefinger or pinky closer to your other fingers so that the spacing is consistent from finger to finger.

Why are my stitches really inconsistent?

If you pull too hard on any given loop around your finger, it will pull other parts of the stitches tight. Try to keep consistent tension as you lift each stitch. Make sure that you are lifting the strands in the correct order, from pinky to forefinger.

What if I dropped a stitch?

Sometimes this happens—it's okay! Remove the stitches from your fingers. Spread the finger-knit strand apart so it is easier to see the purl side from the knit side. Pull out the rows until you reach the row with the dropped stitch. Put all the stitches back on your fingers. If this is difficult, with the purl side of the strand facing up, pull on the working yarn slowly. As this pulling reveals a loop from the prior row, put the loop on your finger. Do this until the working yarn ends up coming from between your forefinger and middle finger.

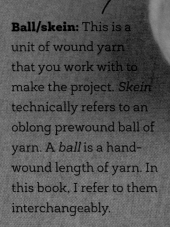

Ball/skein: This is a unit of wound yarn that you work with to make the project. *Skein* technically refers to an oblong prewound ball of yarn. A *ball* is a hand-wound length of yarn. In this book, I refer to them interchangeably.

Strands combined and held: This indicates any number of strands, coming from individual balls, held together to create the working yarn—in this case, three strands.

Stitch: In arm knitting, this is a loop on your arm. Stitches are made by interlocking loops of yarn.

Working yarn: The yarn you are using (typically combined yarn in arm knitting), which extends to your ball(s) of yarn, to make the stitches in your project is the working yarn.

Row: This results each time all the stitches are created and the knit work moves completely from one arm to the other.

Arm Knitting 101

Arm knitting is not all that different from traditional knitting. The technique simply uses your arms as if they were needles to create a series of loops strung together. For people wanting to learn to knit, this is a great way to start because there are no needles to fumble around with at the same time! The biggest difference from traditional knitting is that you cannot turn your arms around, so you are always working from one side of the fabric as opposed to both sides.

Front Leg: Every stitch as two "legs," a right and a left, that straddle your arm. In arm knitting, the "left" leg of the stitch (shown) should always be in front on your right arm, whereas the "right" leg should always be in front on your left arm. On either side, the leg that is in front, the "front leg," should extend directly to the working yarn.

Knit side: The side of the fabric that shows you the knit stitches (stitches that look like a "V"), this is sometimes referred to as the "right side," or the side facing you.

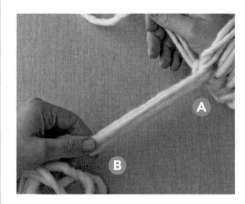

Cast-on stitches (A)

These are the initial armful of stitches created according to the pattern instructions (Casting On, page 162).

Tail (B)

This is the length of yarn used to create the initial set of cast-on stitches.

Casting On

Before you start arm knitting, you need to cast on stitches. This creates anchor loops on your arm from which you will start knitting. Each pattern will indicate how many stitches to cast on.

Casting on uses 2 lengths of the multi-stranded yarn at the same time, the working yarn (which extends to the balls of yarn you are using) and the tail (which extends from the work to the cut end of yarn). Generally, it takes at least 1 yard (0.9m) of tail for every 10 stitches cast on your arm. To be safe, for every 10 stitches, I leave 1½ yards (1.4m) of tail length.

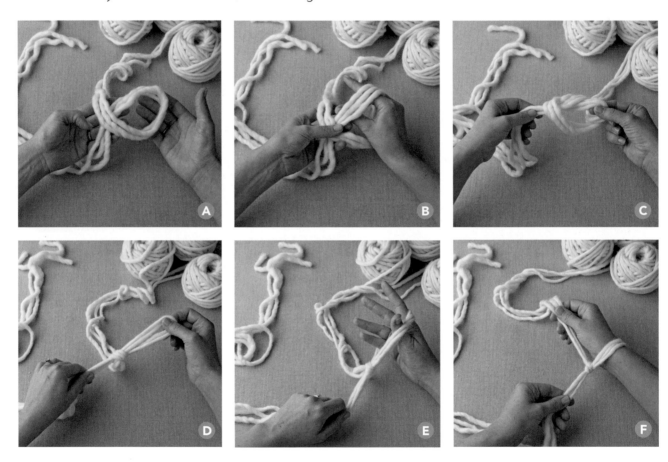

Making the Slip Knot
Leaving enough tail to cast on the required stitches for your project, make a loop by bringing the working yarn over the tail (**A**). Reach through that loop with your right hand (**B**). Bring the working yarn through the loop (**C**) and pull tight (**D**). You have just created a *slip knot*. Place the slip knot on your right arm with the tail closer to you and the working yarn farther from you (**E**). Pull the tail and working yarn apart from each other to tighten (**F**). The slip knot counts as the first cast-on stitch.

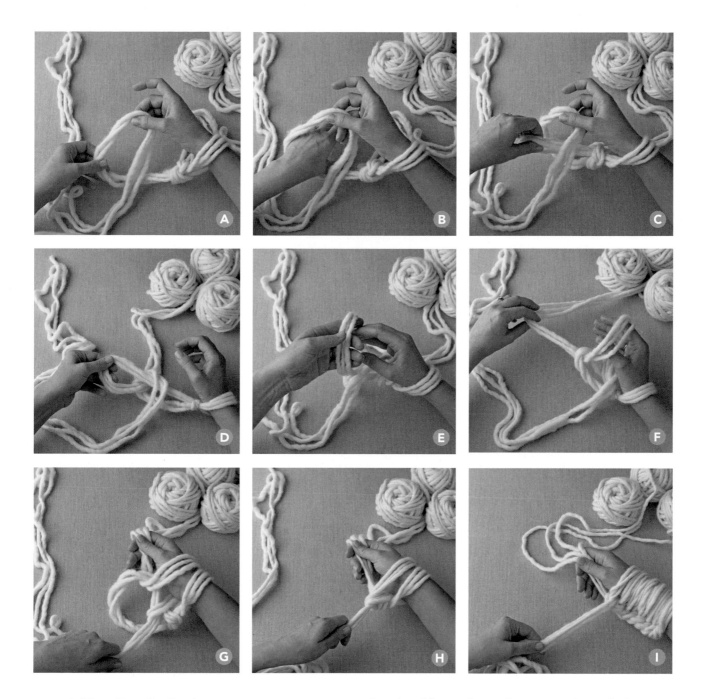

Adding Cast-On Stitches

To continue casting on, make a loop with the tail so that the remainder of the tail hangs in front of the loop (**A**). Hold the top of the loop with your right hand. Put your left hand through the loop (**B**) and grab the working yarn (**C**). Let go of the loop with your right hand and bring the working yarn through the loop (**D**). Put that loop on your right hand (**E, F**). Pull the tail and working yarn apart from each other to tighten the loop on your right arm (**G, H, I**). Repeat A through I for as many stitches as you want or the pattern calls for.

Knitting

Row 1: From now on, ignore the tail. You will be using only the working yarn. Pick up the working yarn and place it over your thumb on your right hand (**A**). Close your fist over the yarn (**B**). Keeping the working yarn in your fist, pull the first stitch (**C**) from your right arm over your fist, effectively pulling the working yarn through that stitch (**D**). Next, drop that old stitch (**E**). Take the new stitch in your right hand, turn the loop a half turn toward you, and place it on your left hand (**F, G**). Another way to think about it is to bring your left hand underneath your right thumb, moving away from you and through the loop. The front leg of the stitch on your hand should be going to the working yarn.

The second stitch is no different than the first, but sometimes it helps to see it twice. (**I, J, K, L**).

Repeat this stitch process until you get to the end of the row. .

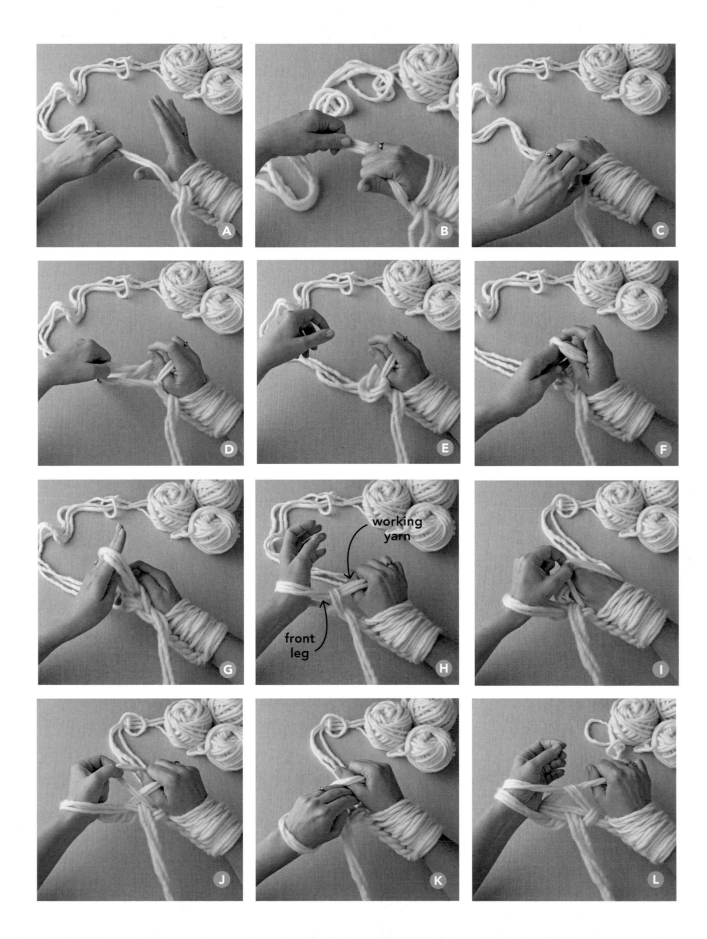

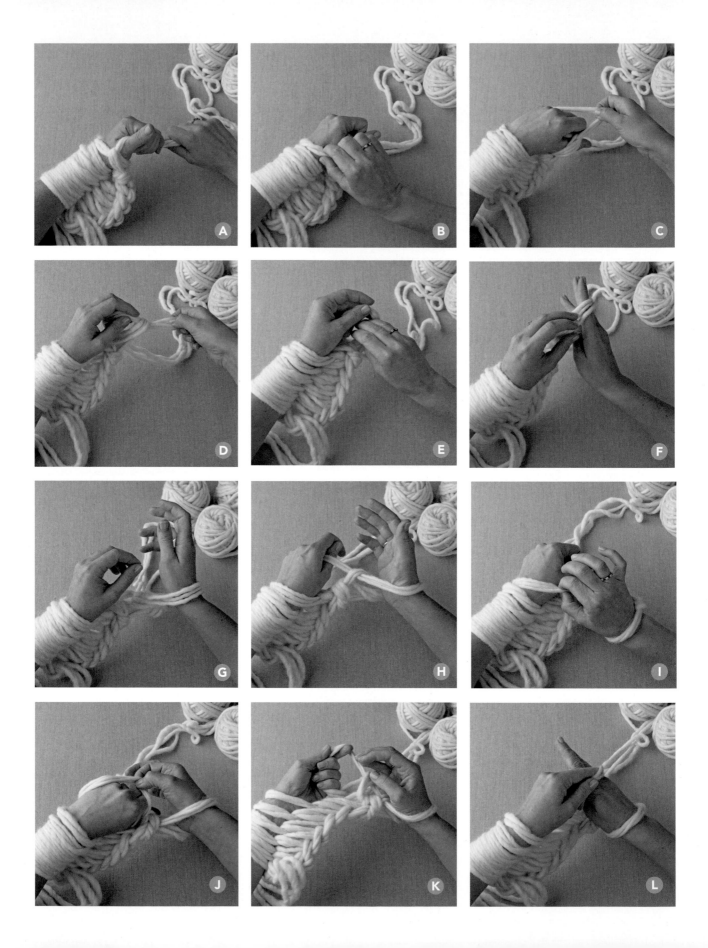

Row 2: Working row 2 is no different than row 1. You are just knitting in the other direction, from your left arm to your right. Place the working yarn over your thumb on your left hand and close your fist (**A**). With your right hand, pull the first stitch from your left arm (**B**) up and over your left fist (**C**). Drop the old stitch from your right hand, keeping hold of the working yarn that is in your left hand (**D**). Put your right hand through the loop in your left hand (**E, F**), turning the stitch slightly so that the working yarn is coming from the front leg of the stitch, and tighten (**G, H**).

The second stitch is the same as the first. Repeat this process until you get to the end of the row (**I, J, K, L**).

Stopping in the Middle

People always ask me, "Do you have to finish your project in one sitting?" The answer is no. It's quite easy to stop anytime along the way.

To stop in the middle of your work, simply put the stitches on a holder of some sort, preferably something that is similar to the size of your arm, like a paper-towel roll (**A**).

You can also use a scrap piece of yarn, a cord, a ruler, wrapping-paper tube, a rolling pin, and so on. Simply pull the stitches from your arm onto the holder (**B**). Leave and do what you need to do (**C**). When you come back, put the stitches back on your arm, remembering that the knit side, or right side, should face you and the working yarn should end up at your hand.

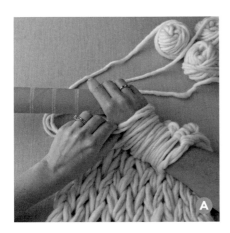

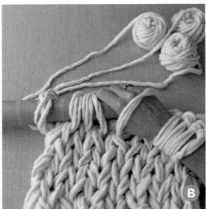

Binding Off

When you have finished knitting, you need to remove the stitches that have been on your arm and secure them so they don't unravel. You will do this by slipping each stitch over the next adjacent stitch and creating a finished edge called the bind off.

. . . .

Note: Bind off loosely. When binding off, keep the stitches loose enough to match the width of the stitches below them.

. . . .

Start with all the stitches on either arm— you can bind off either way. (The photos show binding off from the right arm to the left.) Knit 2 stitches onto your left arm normally. Pick up the first stitch on your left arm (A) and bring it over the last stitch you put on your arm (B, C). Leaving 1 stitch on your left arm, knit the next stitch normally (D, E). There should be 2 stitches on your left arm again. Pull the first stitch over the last

one you put on (F); 1 stitch will be remaining on your left arm (G). Repeat D through G until you get to the last stitch. Remove this stitch from your arm (H) and pull the working yarn through that loop (I). Cut the working yarn or leave enough length as required by your specific project.

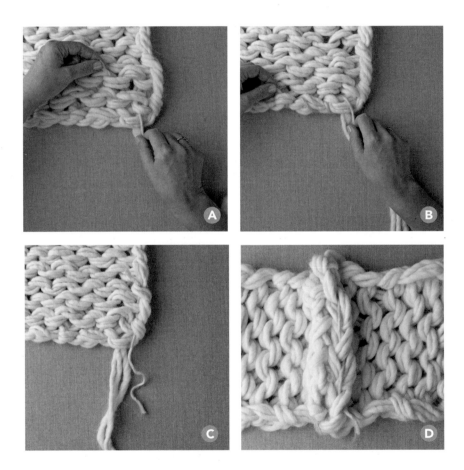

Weaving in Ends

Here are four different ways to weave in ends at the end of a project. The weaving is shown in pink yarn so you can see where the yarn has gone. The method to use depends on the project and fabric you've made and where you want to hide the ends. When you

weave in ends, you can follow the lines of the stitches (A), weave around the end of your fabric (B), work up the side of your fabric (C), or weave into the seam of your fabric (D). If you are nervous about the end coming out, you can knot it to the fabric, but I find this simply makes something bulkier to hide.

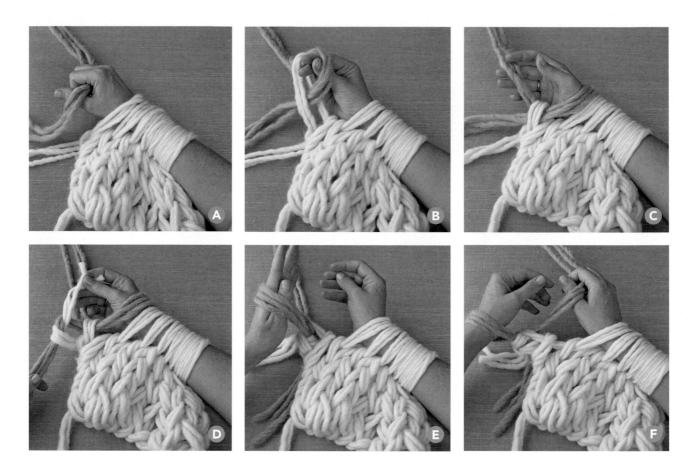

Changing Colors or Adding a New Skein

Use these steps whether you are changing colors or run out of yarn. First, stop knitting at the end of a row and leave your current working yarn to the side. Bring either the new color or the new set of skeins to your hand, leaving an 8" (20.5cm) tail. Pull the first stitch over the new yarn (**A, B**), but instead of transferring the stitch to your other hand, bring the new stitch back over your hand momentarily with all the remaining stitches (**C**). Cut your old working yarn to 8" (20.5cm), unless you will be using the length to seam something later. Tie the two ends together in a knot to secure (**D**). Transfer the first stitch you made back to your other hand (**E**). Continue to knit with the new yarn (**F**).

There is another way to add yarn to a project: Use a sliding knot (see Appendix, page 187) to join individual strands of yarn, one old and one new. It is best if these joins are staggered when using multiple strands of yarn as they will be easier to hide. Use this technique when you don't want the bulk and bother of weaving in two ends, as the sliding knots can easily be hidden among the stitches.

tips and best practices

» To keep the fabric looking full, try to make the stitches as tight as you can while still being able to maneuver. This gets easier in the later rows.

One way to keep stitches tighter is to grab the working yarn close to your hand for the next stitch. Also, you can tighten the stitches as you knit. Start a few stitches away from your hand and pull the leg of the stitch on the back of your arm. Do this on the next stitch closer to your hand, and then the next, scooting the extra length toward the working yarn. Don't make it too tight though! They should be comfortably snug on your arm, but still easy to move.

» When knitting, grab the working yarn near the prior stitch and keep your hands close together as you knit to minimize the amount of excess yarn in any given stitch.

» Wind balls with individual strands only, not multiple strands together. This prevents the yarn from twisting, and it will look nicer when it's knit.

» Make sure the front leg of each stitch (the part of the stitch in front of your hand) goes to the working yarn; otherwise the stitches will twist when the next row is completed.

» Don't pull the stitches too tightly as you bind off. Try to make the stitches match the stitches in the row below.

Beyond Arm Knitting Basics

Once you master the elements of arm knitting, you'll want to learn other stitches and knitting techniques to create almost any kind of project—you're only limited by your imagination!

How to Purl

A purl stitch, which looks like a bump, is simply the reverse side of a knit stitch. When you knit a regular stitch, you simultaneously create a purl stitch on the back side. The purl side is thus sometimes referred to as the "wrong side" or the side facing away from you. Sometimes a pattern will require you to create a purl on the front side (facing you.)

Tip: Arm knitting is different from traditional knitting in that the same side of the fabric always faces you. In traditional knitting, you always knit from the right to the left and turn the work around once you finish a row.

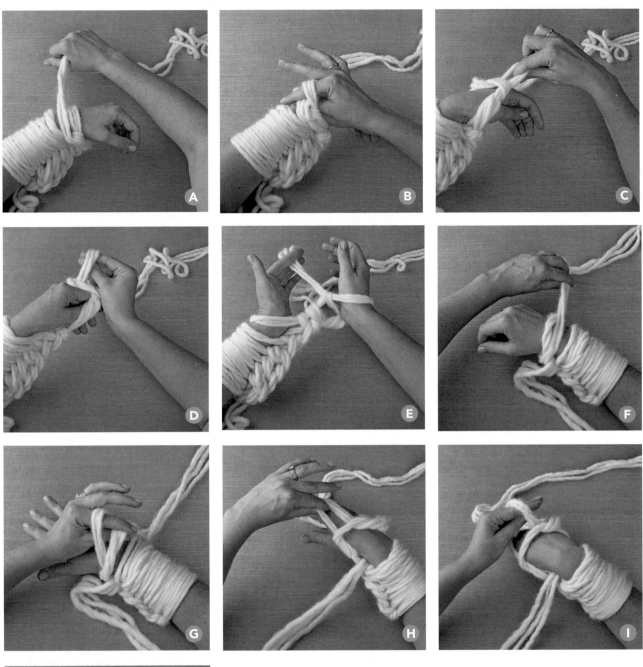

This series of photos shows a purl stitch as you move from the left arm to the right (**A–E**) and from the right arm to the left (**F–J**). Begin by bringing the working yarn right behind the first stitch on your arm (**A**) and let it rest there. Reach through the first stitch and grab the working yarn (**B**). Bring a loop of the working yarn through that stitch (**C**) while pulling that first stitch off your hand. Turn the loop toward you and insert your hand through the loop, moving your hand away from your body (**D**). The working yarn should extend from the front leg of the stitch (**E**). Tighten. Repeat for each purl stitch in the row.

Increasing a Stitch

An increase in knitting is a way of adding a stitch to a row and making the row wider. Increases are a way to shape the fabric to your specified use. When working a pattern that has increases, it helps to keep track of your stitch count to make sure you're increasing when you're supposed to. The pattern will remind you how many stitches you should have as you go.

To increase by knitting into the stitch below at the beginning of a row, make the first stitch as you usually would (**A**). For the second stitch, reach through the stitch below the row you are working on and the stitch you just made (**B**) and grasp the working yarn (**C**). Pull a loop of the working yarn through that old stitch (**D**). Put that loop on to your hand (**E**). Continue to knit the rest of the row as planned.

To increase a stitch at the end of the row by knitting into the stitch below, stop when there is one stitch remaining in the row. Reach through the stitch below the last stitch you made, grab the working yarn, and pull a loop of the working yarn through it. Put that new loop onto your arm as an increased stitch. Knit the last stitch as you normally would. (See Faux Sheepskin, page 85, for photos.)

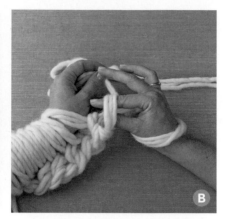

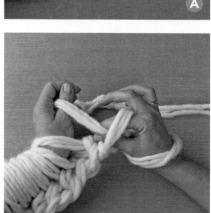

Decreasing a Stitch (Knit 2 Together)

Decreasing a stitch reduces the overall number of stitches on your arm and makes the row narrower. This specific decrease is known as "knitting 2 stitches together," or abbreviated as "k2tog."

To decrease a stitch, begin as if you are completing a regular stitch, but bring the first 2 stitches on your arm (A) over the working yarn (B). Move that new stitch to your other hand (C). You can accomplish this decrease at any point along the row; the photos show it at the beginning of a row.

Garter Stitch

Knit 1 row and then purl 1 row. Continue to alternate to create this plush, springy fabric.

Lattice Lace Stitch

For a lacy effect, you can create an open space in your stitch work by increasing stitches and decreasing in a special pattern. For directions, see Lace Pillows (page 81).

Stockinette Stitch (Purl Side)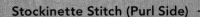

The flip side of stockinette stitch is known as the purl side. If you wanted the purl side of the fabric to face you as you knit, you would have to purl (see page 172) every stitch, both directions.

Stockinette Stitch (Knit Side)

In arm knitting, the easiest pattern stitch is stockinette. To create it, you simply knit in both directions, from your right arm to your left and from your left arm to your right. The side facing you is the knit side.

Moss Stitch

This effect is created by alternately knitting 1 stitch and purling 1 stitch. On the next row, you alternate the stitches again, purling on top of the stitch where you knit, and knitting on top of the stitch where you purled. Continue to alternate stitches each row. It is easier to cast on an even number of stitches so you can always start each row with a knit stitch.

Seaming and Finishing

At the end of an arm-knitting project, you often need to sew or seam pieces together to finish the project. Additionally, there are ways to add a final touch to your project to give it that finished look. Sometimes you cut a new length of yarn to do these tasks. Sometimes, you can use the tail from the cast-on edge or a length left over from binding off. The pattern will specify which is best.

Blocking

Blocking is a good idea if you are completing a piece to wear, if you want a piece to be a certain size, or if your piece consists of a more complex stitch pattern, like the Lace Pillows (page 81). The blocking process allows you to shape a knit piece to a desired size. It relaxes the fibers that you've knit and evens out stitches.

To block a piece, submerge it in cool water. Let it sit for up to an hour to absorb the water. Do not agitate the piece, especially if it's knit with 100 percent wool. Gently squeeze out the excess water; do not wring or twist. Lay the piece on a large bath towel and roll the towel up from the bottom. Let the towel absorb even more water. Then, lay the piece out on a blocking board or on a clean carpeted area. Pin the piece down with rustproof T-pins to the desired size and shape. For example, if making the Lace Pillows, pin the piece to match the pillow form you are fitting inside. Let dry completely.

Slip Stitch Finishing

A slip-stitch edging provides a nice finish, especially if the piece is knit in stockinette stitch, which tends to curl at the edges. This technique is used in the Rope Rug (page 65) and the Cabled Blanket (page 92).

Start by bringing a loop of your border yarn through the middle of the outermost stitch along the edge of your work (A). With your fingers, reach through this loop and the next stitch along the edge of the work (B). Grab the working yarn and pull a new loop of yarn through the old loop (C). Repeat that process along the edge of your fabric, working stitch for stitch (D). When you get to the end of the side, complete an extra stitch in the last stitch to help you turn the corner (E). Continue along the end, making a slip stitch in between each end stitch; there should be as many slip stitches along the end as cast-on stitches (F).

. . . .

Tip: If you are slip stitching in the same color as your work, you likely won't need to slip stitch along the bound-off edge as those stitches look very similar to a slip stitch border.

. . . .

Garter Stitch Edging

Another way to keep a knit edge from rolling is to knit a piece with a garter stitch edge (see Arm-Knitting Stitch Patterns, page 180). This would be perfect for a large knit blanket. Create this edge while you are arm knitting, not after, by purling 2 or 3 stitches at the beginning and end of each row, alternated with knitting those same 2 stitches at the beginning and end of the next row.

Slip Stitch Seaming

The slip stitch can be used to seam two pieces of arm knitting together to make a beautiful contrasting edge or to add a firm border, as in the Purl-Side Tote (page 53).

Begin by facing two pieces with wrong sides together (**A**). Line the pieces up stitch for stitch, and bring a loop of your working yarn through the first pair of stitches, one from each piece (**B**). Reach through this first loop and the second pair of stitches, grab the working yarn (**C**), and bring it through this group, making a second loop or slip stitch (**D**). Repeat this process for every stitch along both edges. Make an extra stitch in the corner (**E**). When seaming along the end, go in between each stitch (**F**). You can see how slip stitch seaming holds the sides of the two pieces together, while providing a pretty edging at the same time.

• •

Tip: As you seam or finish a piece, try not to pull the seaming or finishing so tight that it gathers the stitches along the edge of your piece. Keep the seams relaxed so that one piece matches the width of the other. Keep your slip stitch loose enough that it matches the width of your fabric.

• •

Mattress Seaming End to End
To join the bound-off and cast-on edges of an arm-knit piece, use this virtually invisible seam.

   With the right sides of your fabric facing you (the knit side or purl side), line the pieces up end to end and matched stitch for stitch (A). Bring the seaming yarn (whether it's new yarn or leftover working yarn or a tail from the project) under and around the first stitch or V shape on the left-hand edge, then go under and around the first stitch or V shape on the right-hand side (B). Alternate your seaming stitches from side to side (C). You can leave the seaming stitches loose enough to make them look like another row of stitches, or you can pull the seaming strand taut (but not too tight!) and bring the edges together (D).

Mattress Seaming Side to Side
This invisible seam is used in the Oversized Pillows (page 61) and the Pom-Pom (page 32), Beanie (page 45), and Slouch (page 40) Hats.

   With the right sides of your fabric facing you, line the pieces up side by side, stitch for stitch (A). Bring your seaming yarn under the bottom of the first stitch on the left-hand edge, then go under the bottom of the first stitch on the right-hand side (B). Alternate your seaming stitches from side to side (C). Pull taut (D).

Arm-Knitting Yarn Preparation

In most arm-knitting projects you'll be plying yarn, or combining and holding multiple strands of yarn together to make a bulkier yarn with which to work. Because of the changing amount of yardage in each project and the varying amount of yardage in yarn skeins, some measuring and splitting of skeins will make your projects more cost-effective. Here are a few project scenarios that illustrate different ways to split a skein.

» A project requires the entire yardage of a skein or ball of yarn. For example, your project requires a total of 270 yards (247m) of yarn, plying three 90-yard (82m) strands at a time. If your balls are approximately 100 yards (91.4m) each, you can simply arm knit directly from the separate skeins—no splitting necessary.

» A project requires less yarn than available in a skein, For example, your project requires a total 180 yards (160m), plying six 30-yard (27.5m) strands at a time. If your skeins contain 90 yards (82m) each, you can split two skeins into three 30-yard (27.5m) lengths, and then ply those six strands together for your project.

» A project requires more yardage provided than one set of skeins plyed together, but doesn't require enough yardage to use an additional set of skeins. For example, your project requires a total of 375 yards (344m), plying three 125-yard (114m) lengths, but you only have 100 yard (91.4m) skeins. Arm knit directly from three skeins of yarn, and split the fourth skein into three 30-yard (27.5m) lengths to complete the project.

Three Ways to Split a Skein
1. If I know I will have to stop mid project, I measure and wind each length of yarn into separate balls. With a ruler or measuring tape, measure and cut one "guide strand" to be the length you need. Proceed by

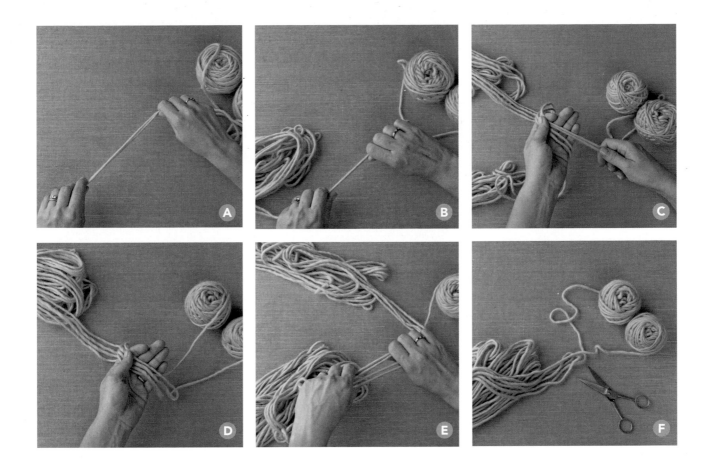

measuring each strand you need individually against the guide strand. Take the time to wrap each individual length into its own ball. Don't wind multiple strands together into a ball as they can get super twisted.

2. If you have a precise scale, you can split a skein directly in half or thirds or fourths by weight. Divide the total skein weight in ounces or grams by the number you are splitting it into and wind individual balls to that weight.

3. If you know you will complete your project in one sitting and won't need to move your pile, I find it faster and easier to split the skeins by pulling the lengths into piles of plied yarns. Here's an example of how to split two skeins into six strands.

With two strands in your hand (**A**), measure the required length, running the yarn through your hands as you go. You can measure with a yardstick or measuring tape. For ease, you may want to figure out a personal physical reference to measure a yard; for me, it's from my shoulder down the length of my arm. As you measure, pull the two strands into an organized pile (**B**). When you get the desired length, start quadrupling the length of yarn, pulling from the length you just made and the balls of yarn at the same time (**C**). When you get to the end of the first set of two strands plied together (**D**), start plying another two strands to get to six strands making an organized pile as you go (**E**). When you get to the end of the set of four strands, cut the last two strands (**F**). Then, arm knit directly from the pile.

Troubleshooting Arm Knitting

As easy as arm knitting is, you'll inevitably have a few hiccups along the way. It takes practice to master a new craft. You can do it! Hopefully these tips and solutions on will help.

Adjusting Yarn Gauge

Yarn gauge is dependent on yarn weight but also on the tool used to make the stitches, in this case, your arms. The size of your arms will affect your fabric: 10 stitches knit on my daughter's arms will be smaller than 10 stitches knit on mine. The looseness with which you knit can also affect gauge. In most projects in this book—the Infinity Cowl (page 13), Rope Rug (page 65), Faux Sheepskin (page 85), and Cabled Blanket (page 92), for example—it won't matter if your fabric is a couple inches wider or narrower than the measurements listed.

To minimize the margin of error, pay attention to the category of yarn and the range of stitches per inch that your yarn falls into (see page 142). These categories will help your project be similar in size and shape to the project in the photo.

If you're concerned about something fitting or being a certain size, make a test swatch by casting on 10 stitches and arm knitting 10 rows. Measure how many stitches you get over 10" (25.5cm) and divide by 10 to determine how many stitches to each inch you are knitting. Compare that to the stitches per inch for the fabric gauge in the pattern. You can calculate this by dividing the number of stitches by the finished measurements of the piece. In traditional knitting, if your gauge differs from a pattern, you would simply change your needle size up or down to get the required number of stitches per inch. In arm knitting, here are your options.

If you have *fewer* stitches per inch than the pattern gauge, your fabric will be bigger; you can:

» Decrease the bulkiness of the yarn (if loose knitting is the problem, then this won't help)
» Arm knit tighter (but don't hurt yourself! See Frequently Asked Questions, below, for tips).

If you have *more* stitches per inch than the pattern gauge, your fabric will be smaller; you can:

» Increase the bulkiness of the yarn
» Arm knit looser

If the options above don't work, you can adjust the number of stitches in order to achieve the measurements given in the pattern.

Frequently Asked Questions

Why are my stitches too loose?

The best way to control the size of the stitches is to minimize the size of each loop of yarn pulled through any stitch. Grab the working yarn close to your hand for the next stitch and keep the amount of yarn pulled through for the next stitch to a minimum. Keep your hands close together as you knit (though you should still be able to move your hands). You can also tighten the stitches manually, bringing any excess length from stitches into the working yarn. If you do this, keep the stitches a consistent size, snug on your arm but not tight.

Or, potentially, the yarn you are using may not be thick enough to create a substantial yarn. Try adding an additional strand for your project and see if that helps.

Why are my edge stitches messed up?

A certain level of irregularity at the edges (a bigger edge stitch followed by a smaller edge stitch) is normal because of the arm knitting process. In many projects the edge will be seamed into the middle or the edge will curl, and folks won't see it. Sometimes you just end up with one or two bigger stitches here and there. As long as the stitch count is okay, you can even out some of this distortion by hand after you bind off. You also can add a slip-stitch edging (page 179).

Why do my stitches have a twist in them?

Make sure you are adding the extra turn in the stitch as you pull the working yarn through to put it on your arm. Your hand needs to go through the stitch away from your body. Remember, the front leg of the stitch (the part of the stitch in front of your arm) should lead directly to the working yarn.

Why is my bound-off edge wider than my cast-on edge (or vice versa)?

The size of the bound-off edge is controlled by you as each prior stitch is pulled over the new stitch. Bind off loosely (or more tightly, as necessary) so that the bound-off stitches are the same width as the stitches below them.

The cast-on edge will typically be tighter than the worked stitches above it. Adjust this by pulling along the cast-on edge to the desired width. Don't pull too much, though, because it's harder to tighten it back up!

Why are my stitches inconsistent?

The higher the number of stitches on your arm, the more likely stitch size will become inconsistent (our arms aren't perfect cylinders!). If you have a lot of stitches on your arm, you can even out the size of the stitches after you've bound off. Pull some of the additional length in the longer stitches to the edges where the smaller, tighter edge stitches have room to expand.

What if I dropped a stitch?

Don't panic. Bring the work to a flat table so that the weight of the work doesn't pull the stitches out farther. Remove the stitches from your arm and slowly pull the working yarn, undoing the stitches until you reach the row with the dropped stitch. From there, undo an additional row, placing each revealed stitch from the row below onto a holder (such as a paper-towel or gift-wrap tube) as the working yarn is pulled out. When you reach the end of the row, place the entire set of stitches back on your arm, making sure that the working yarn ends up near your hand.

I put the stitches on a holder. How do I figure out where I am?

Find the right side of the fabric. If you are knitting, then the knit side (page 161) should be facing you. Next, the working yarn should end up at your hand. For example, if the working yarn is on the left side of the work, put the stitches on your right arm.

APPENDIX

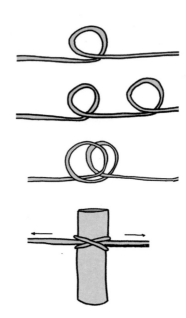

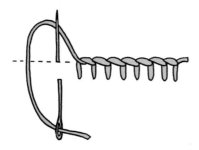

Blanket Stitch

Blanket stitch is a decorative edging that can also be used to seam two edges together in a pretty way. At its most simple, the blanket stitch is created in this way: as you bring your needle through the fabric from front to back for each stitch, you catch the loop of your thread from the former stitch along the top of the fabric. Specifically, begin by bringing a knotted thread through your fabric, back to front, ¼" from the edge. (Leave a little room in this initial stitch, which will stay wonky until you come back around to it.) Make your next stitch ⅛" to the side of your last stitch, moving the needle from the front to the back (also ¼" in from the edge) and inserting your needle through the loop of your thread. Pull your stitch taut. Continue to repeat this stitch, moving from your right to your left. When you get back to where you started, create your last stitch, bringing the needle through your first stitch to create the last blanket stitch.

Clove Hitch

Make two loops in your yarn or thread going in the same direction. Cross and overlap the loops, bringing the loop of the topmost strand underneath the prior loop in the series. Bring overlapping loops on top of what you want to secure and tighten.

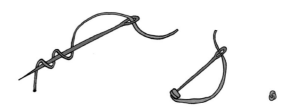

French Knot

Insert your needle from the wrong to the right side. Keeping the thread taut with one hand, use your other hand to wind the yarn over needle twice. Reinsert the tip of needle into the fabric, as close as possible to where it emerged (but not through the same hole). Before pulling the needle through the fabric, pull the thread tight so the knot is flush with the fabric. Pull all the way through to finish the knot.

Sliding Knot

A sliding knot will help secure two ends of yarn. Start by taking the end of yarn (**A**) and knot it around the length of yarn (**B**), bringing the end of yarn A through two loops to secure it. Next, take yarn B end and repeat the knot around the length of yarn A. Then pull the lengths of A and B apart from one another until the knots slide together. Trim ends.

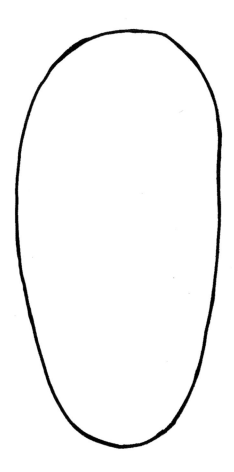

Bootie Template

Trace pattern and cut two bootie pieces from felt.

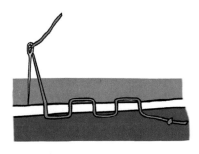

Blind Stitch

Use a blind stitch to seam two folded pieces of fabric together so that the stitches are invisible. (Rather than sewing the outside pieces of the fabric together, you'll be working on the inside folds of the fabric.) First, secure your thread by inserting the needle and knotted thread between the two pieces of fabric and into the inside of the folded fabric nearest you. Then catch the inside fold of the other piece of fabric and run the needle and thread through that channel for ¼". Next, insert the needle and thread into the folded fabric nearest you and run the needle and thread through that channel for ¼". Repeat this process across the entire length of your opening.

RESOURCES

A big thank-you to **Purl Soho**, who generously supplied all the beautiful yarn for this book, www.purlsoho.com.

The following lovingly loaned me beautiful items for the photo shoots, including:

Creative Thursday, www.creativethursday.com: Eiffel Tower painting

Le Train Fantome, www.letrainfantome.com: Lumi doll

Bryr Studio, www.bryrstudio.com: Clogs on models

QP Collections, www.qpcollections: Tree house location and other props

Pam Morris, www.pammorrisstyle.com: Various props

Brittany Jepsen, www.thehousethatlars built.com: Various props

Materials by Project:
Double-Strand Headband: Cotton ribbon from Studio Cartam, www.angelaliguori.com

Grand Pouf: King-sized alternative down comforter from www.amazon.com

Hemp Twine Necklace: Hemp 3-strand twine from Crochet Hemp, www.crochethemp.com; glass button from Woolworks, www.wool works.com

Jump Rope: Antique handles and beads from Etsy, www.etsy.com; macrame cord from Michael's

Lace Pillows: Fabric from Purl Soho, www.purlsoho.com; sewing notions from Joann's

Octopus Family: Button eyes from Woolworks, www.woolworks.com; fabric from Purl Soho, www.purlsoho.com, and Joann's

Oversized Pillow: European 26" square pillows from Overstock, www.overstock.com; cover fabrics and sewing notions from Joann's

Prince and Princess Crown: Wire and crystal beads from Michael's

Purl-Side Tote: Chicago bolts, leather strapping, leather cord, rotary punch from Outfitters Supply Inc., www.outfitterssupply.com; liner fabrics, interfacing, and sewing notions from Joann's

Reading Nook: Cabone ring, Darice 23" quilting hoop from Amazon.com; ribbon, 6" tulle, and novelty beads from Joann's

Rope Rug: ¼" (6mm) cotton rope from Knot and Rope Supply, www.knotandrope.com

Statement Necklace: Chain, jump rings, clasp from Michael's

Two-Tone Dog Collar: Macrame cord from Michael's; brass buckle from Dog Walkies, www.etsy.com/shop/dogwalkies

Wired Word: Wire from Michael's

Woven Rug: 32" x 40" Nielsen Bainbridge dual color mat board from Utrecht Art Supplies, www.utrechtart.com; warp thread from Crochet Hemp, www.crochethemp.com

ACKNOWLEDGMENTS

THANK YOU

To Allie, for her endless creativity and natural joy, especially for that fateful night we brainstormed finger-knitting projects when this book was merely a spark. To Charlie and Baillie, who put up with the stress and provide kindness and tenderness when I need it. To Sandy, who every day makes me feel loved, supported, and whole. To Kat McIver, loyal friend, advisor, and Mom, who thankfully was never far from her phone. To Joanne Torres, sister-in-law extraordinaire, for her magnanimous and bright spirit and for her time and incomparable skill with language. To my talented friends Brittany Watson Jepsen, Lizzy House, Lisa Congdon, Betz White, Camille DeAngeles, and Amy Gamper, for their advice, faith, and support, felt from near and far.

To all the brave pioneering pattern testers, good work! To Stefanie Von Borstel, who encouraged me (and so many others) to really go for it. To Caitlin Harpin, who amazes me with her tireless patience and simple way with words. To Angelin Borsics, who jumped in and picked up the reins with aplomb. To Brittany Watson Jepsen (again!) and Pam Morris, for their commitment to my aesthetic and their own lovely style. To Jessica Peterson, for her amazing ability to get a face. To Lucy Schaeffer, for her dedication to showing these projects in their best light. To talented Trisha Zemp, my step-by-step photographer, for, well, she knows exactly what for—she has my undying gratitude.

To these gorgeous models who generously gave of their time and energy to help make this book: Michelle Christensen, Morgan Sidwell, Kassidy Walker, Kera Thompson, Quinn Peterson, Lydia Black, Macy Trapnell, Creed Ford, and Georgia Lee. To those that helped them look their best and most beautiful: Vivian Johnson, Sarah Thompson and Callie Stott. To photo and styling assistants Justin Miller, Brynn Grover, Victoria Riza, Carli, Yendi Reid, Biz Jones, and Sophie Strangio. To the rest of the skilled and hardworking staff at Potter Craft, including Stephanie Huntwork, Ian Dingman, Jessie Bright, Ada Yonenaka, Heather Williamson, Hanna Glidden, Natasha Martin, and Lauren Velasquez. To Karen Brook for her thorough and careful read. To Lucy, my trusty dog and studio mate, for her hearty tail wags and hugs when I need them most.

Lastly, to my readers and fans, who have supported my blog and my creativity through the years, which gratefully, made this entire book possible.

INDEX